The HITLER Conspiracies

The HITLER Conspiracies

Secrets and Lies behind the Rise and Fall of the Nazi Party

DAVID WELCH

BRASSEY'S, INC.

Washington, D.C.

First published in the United States of America by
Brassey's, Inc.
22841 Quicksilver Drive
Dulles, Virginia 20166

Copyright © 2001 Brown Partworks Limited

ISBN 1-57488-380-1

Brassey's books are available at special discounts for bulk purchases
for sales promotions, fund raising or educational use.

First Edition
10 9 8 7 6 5 4 3 2 1

Editorial and design:
Brown Partworks Ltd
8 Chapel Place
Rivington Street
London
EC2A 3DQ
UK

Editor: Anne Cree
Picture research: Susannah Jayes
Design: Mike Lebihan
Production: Matt Weyland

Printed in Singapore

CONTENTS

HITLER'S RISE TO POWER

Hitler liked to portray his rise to power as being meteoric, but it was actually haphazard and owed a lot to luck. And behind the scenes establishment figures conspired to bring the Nazis to power.

There was nothing inevitable about the triumph of Adolf Hitler and his party, the NSDAP. His rise to power was perfectly resistible. His early life provides little indication of a precocious talent or of the

Members of the *Stosstrupp-Hitler*, the bodyguard of the leader of the right-wing National Socialist German Workers' Party (NSDAP), in Munich during the abortive November 1923 Beer Hall Putsch. Note the swastika armbands.

demagogic leader that was to have such a profound impact on the world stage. In 1923, when he was jailed for the abortive Munich Putsch, the Bavarian authorities ought to have imprisoned him for longer and on his release he should have been deported to Austria. Had this happened it is very difficult to see how he could have resurrected his political career. He would have been finished as a political figure in Germany. Moreover, as late as 1928, Hitler and the Nazis were still peripheral political forces,

> ## *The young Hitler was hostile to his authoritarian father, and strongly devoted to his mother*

and in the elections of that year were rejected by 97 percent of the electorate. Even when he was appointed Chancellor in March 1933, 56 percent of voters still rejected him.

Adolf Hitler was born in Braunau am Inn, Austria (on the Austrian border with Germany), on 20 April 1889. The son of a stuffy 52-year-old customs official, Alois Schickelgruber Hitler, and his third wife, a young peasant girl, Klara Poelzl, both from the region of Lower Austria, the young Hitler was hostile to his authoritarian father, and strongly devoted to his protective and indulgent mother.

There is little to suggest anything remarkable about Hitler as a boy. His academic records show that he was not an outstanding student. His school career lasted for 10 years, of which the last four were a struggle. He finally left in September 1905, without taking any final examinations and with a poor report that drew particular attention to his inadequate command of the

Hitler photographed in 1924, following the failure of the Munich Putsch and his imprisonment in Landsberg. Despite its failure, it had given him publicity: "I'm no longer an unknown, and that provides us with the best basis for a new start."

Hitler's doting mother, Klara. Perhaps the only person for whom he ever felt any close affection, her death on 21 December 1907 hit him particularly hard. He himself described it as "a dreadful blow" in *Mein Kampf*.

German language. In Hitler's defence it should be noted that as an adolescent he was disturbed by the deaths of his younger brother Edmund (1900), his father (1903) and his beloved mother (1907). Without delving too deeply into psychological speculation about Hitler's state of mind, some biographers have suggested that these deaths (and his own survival) convinced the future Führer that he was marked out by destiny for a special future.

By 1907, Hitler had moved to Vienna to seek admission to the Academy of Fine Arts. Embittered at his rejection by the Academy, he returned briefly to Linz after the death of his mother. Alone and without an occupation he left for Vienna again. Hitler later described this break with his provincial, middle class past in dramatic

Hitler regarded his authoritarian father, Alois, with less affection, especially as he wanted his son to become a civil servant like himself. This idea filled the young Adolf, who had visions of becoming an artist, with dread.

terms: "With my clothes and linen packed in a valise, and with an indomitable resolution in my heart, I left for Vienna. I hoped to forestall fate, as my father had done some 50 years before. I was determined to become 'something'." He was to spend five years of "misery and woe" in Vienna as he later recalled, leading a bohemian, vagabond existence and generally undergoing an identity crisis.

The young Adolf Hitler (back row, centre), aged 10, in his Leonding school photograph in 1899. His academic record during his youth was poor, and teachers noted his lack of self-discipline, stubborn nature and time-wasting.

Cosmopolitan Vienna helped shape his pathological hatred of Jews and Marxists, and he began to indulge in grandiose dreams of a Greater Germany. Hitler had

German troops in World War I. Upon hearing of the outbreak of war, Hitler later wrote: "I fell down on my knees and thanked Heaven from an overflowing heart for granting me the good fortune of being permitted to live at this time."

become a passionate German nationalist while still at school. Although the dual monarchy of Austria-Hungary gave the impression of stability and permanence, the irreconcilable demands of competing ethnic groups (referred to by Hitler as "bacilli") were already imposing unbearable strains on the Hapsburg Empire and the ageing Emperor Franz Joseph. Hitler despised the ramshackle and multi-national Empire, and fervently believed that it should be ruled by Germans without concessions to the Slavs and other subject peoples. There is an obvious irony in the fact that Hitler's fanatical German nationalism should spring from his Austrian roots. Indeed, many of Hitler's ideas can be traced to turn of the century Austria-Hungary where intense nationalism had even more significance than in Germany itself.

WORLD WAR I

Isolated and unsuccessful in Vienna, Hitler moved to Munich in May 1913 at the age of 24 to avoid service in the Austrian Army. However, at the outbreak of war in August 1914, Hitler enlisted in the 16th Bavarian Infantry Regiment, serving as a despatch runner. He proved a courageous soldier, receiving the Iron Cross for bravery on two occasions, and was promoted to lance-corporal in 1917. Twice wounded, he was badly gassed in October 1918 and spent three months recuperating in a hospital in Pomerania when the Armistice was declared.

At the end of the war, amid considerable revolutionary fervour in Germany, he returned to a Munich undergoing violent political upheavals and joined the DAP (*Deutsche Arbeiterpartei* – German Workers' Party), a counter-revolutionary movement dedicated to the principles of "German national socialism", as opposed to "Jewish Marxism" or Russian Bolshevism. In the summer of 1919 he had been assigned by the *Reichswehr* (German Army) to spy on extremist groups in Munich, and it was as a *Reichswehr* informant that he was sent to monitor the activities of the nationalist and racist DAP, led by the Munich locksmith Anton Drexler. In September 1919, he joined the DAP, which comprised between 20 and 40 members, and on 16 October he made his first address to the Party. He was 30 years old and his political career had just begun. Hitler wrote in his book, *Mein Kampf*: "Generally speaking, a man should not take part in politics before he has reached the age of 30."

> ### *At the end of the war, amid considerable revolutionary fervour, he returned to Munich*

Hitler's task was made easier by the fact that the Weimar Republic was subject to the hostility of both left- and right-wing groups, who actively conspired against it. The left-wing Spartacist Revolt in Berlin in 1919, when workers tried to establish a socialist regime, and the Kapp Putsch of 1920, when the *Freikorps* made a right-wing journalist Chancellor, are but two examples.

Hitler in German Army uniform in 1916. Unsociable to his comrades and having no close friends, the Austrian corporal did not lack for courage: the job of despatch runner was a dangerous one, and earned him the Iron Cross.

In February 1920, the DAP changed its name to the NSDAP (*Nationalsozialistische Deutsche Arbeiterpartei* – National Socialist German Workers' Party) or Nazi for short, and set out its 25-point Party programme. The name at the bottom of the manifesto was not that of Hitler but of Anton Drexler. Although Hitler had only been a member of the Party for a year, the 25 points reveal the influence of his ideas. The programme contained many of the policies that became associated with the Nazis when they gained

Hitler would later claim that his ideas had been firmly established by 1914

power constitutionally in 1933. There are early indications of the eugenics policy that would later be implemented by the Nazis. Interestingly, the programme anticipated a degree of state interventionism that goes beyond the staple *völkisch* ideas of other nationalist groups. War profits and some property were to be confiscated, unearned incomes abolished, trusts nationalized and department stores communalized. Hitler's influence can be seen in the prominence given to the myth of Aryan race supremacy and the exclusion of Jews from the *Volksgemeinschaft* (*Volk* – or national – community).

Although Hitler had presented the programme, which he had partly edited, on 24 February 1920, it had been drawn up largely without his direct help. It is doubtful that Hitler was ever wedded to the 25 points as a philosophical blueprint, viewing it as no more than a means to an end. He had agreed to the programme simply because it reflected the radical anti-capitalism of the time, and

was more likely to attract disenchanted working class and lower middle class support in the beer halls and on the streets of Munich. By the late 1920s, having established himself as leader of the DAP, the "socialistic" ideas of profit sharing and nationalization had become an embarrassment and were explicitly disavowed in an attempt to woo big business and the middle classes in general.

Although Hitler's nationalistic ideas were scarcely distinguishable from those of a plethora of pan-German agitators, his gift

for self-dramatization made an immediate impact in the beer halls of Munich, where he quickly established a reputation as a populist demagogue. Hitler would later claim that his ideas had been firmly established before 1914. While it is true that the core of his obsessive beliefs and prejudices remained constant, in the early to mid-1920s important modifications took place in the crystallization of his own world view. In particular, his anti-Semitism became even more firmly linked to his antipathy towards Marxism – which in his view was its political

Freikorps (groups of right-wing ex-soldiers) members during the crushing of the Munich communist government in 1919. In September of that year, the army employed Hitler to report on the Munich-based German Workers' Party.

and ideological manifestation; his own self-image underwent a process of change; and the geopolitical idea of *Lebensraum (*living space) emerged as a central plank of Germany's future foreign policy.

The experience of war, the humiliation of defeat and the revolutionary unrest in

13

Anton Drexler, the Chairman of the German Workers' Party, the organization that the army sent Hitler to report on in September 1919. Impressed by Drexler's ideas, Hitler joined the party during the second half of September.

Munich all made a profound impression on Hitler, and provided him with opportunities to disseminate his right-wing views. Hitler's arguments did not change appreciably – old nationalistic slogans were repeated and the Jews continued to be blamed for every political setback. Hitler even blamed the loss of World War I on the Jews. However, after the war, the historical hatred of the Jews was increased by the credence given inside the Party to the ideas of a "Jewish world conspiracy". Alfred Rosenberg, later to

> ## "Jewish conspirators were preparing to assume total domination over all nations"

became the guardian of the National Socialist *Weltanschauung* (world view) and leading theoretician of Nazi racism, had introduced Hitler to the forged *Protocols of the Elders of Zion*, according to which an international clique of Jewish conspirators were preparing to assume total domination over all nations of the world. Although the "Protocols" were subsequently proved to be a Tsarist police forgery, Hitler remained convinced of their authenticity to the end of his

Alfred Rosenberg, Nazi "philosopher", addressing a group of workers in 1932. It was Rosenberg who introduced Hitler to the forged *Protocols of the Elders of Zion*, which talked of an international Jewish conspiracy.

days. Hitler's anti-Semitism, which had been an established part of his stock-in-trade, now fused with anti-Marxism into the conviction of an all-embracing worldwide Jewish-Bolshevik conspiracy.

The shift appears to have taken place in the mid-1920s. As a result of the Russian Revolution and Civil War, anti-Marxism assumes an increasingly important focus for his attacks. The Jewish threat is not diminished but there is now a second factor. For Hitler the life-and-death struggle would now focus squarely on the twin evils of Judaism and Marxism. Increasingly the distinction blurred, Jews became synonymous with Bolsheviks and the Jewish-Bolshevik conspiracy was conflated. Hitler concluded from this that Europe was now locked in a racial struggle which only a racially cleansed Germany under his leadership could win.

The First Nazi Party Day in Munich, 28 January 1923. By this time Hitler was Chairman of the Party, having ousted Drexler, and had established a power base in Munich. The Party was also growing steadily, having 3000 members in 1921.

By 1924 a central plank of Hitler's world view was already established: history as a racial struggle against Judaism and its political manifestation, Marxism. Interestingly enough, Hitler's notion of the "heroic Führer-figure" and the need for *Lebensraum* in the east had not yet been fully formulated. All three would eventually fuse into an integral vision whereby the struggle to obtain more *Lebensraum* for Germany at the expense of Russia would lead to an historic showdown with Jewish Bolshevism and end in triumph for the German "master race" under the leadership of an heroic Führer. To the end of his days, Hitler remained convinced that Jewish Bolshevism and Western culture could not co-exist. The only possible outcome was the destruction of one of these forces. For Hitler, the destruction of Marxism and the destruction of the Jews were identical goals – and this was to be the historic task of a "Germanic state of the German nation".

LEBENSRAUM

Hitler's belief in the authenticity of the *Protocols of the Elders of Zion* and the success of "Jewish Bolshevism" in Russia had implications for his thinking on German foreign policy. Hitler's racial philosophy led him to demand *Lebensraum* for Germans, while his adherence to Social Darwinism convinced him that war was a natural part of history and the ultimate test of a nation's spiritual and moral fibre. But where would this *Lebensraum* be found?

Hitler rejected the scramble for colonial acquisitions made by the Kaiser prior to 1914, arguing that such a policy had antagonized Britain and had led to an unnecessary war. He fixed his gaze instead on Eastern Europe and Russia in particular. A war with Soviet Russia, Hitler concluded, would prove attractive to the nations of

Western Europe in their struggle against the insidious threat of Bolshevism. It would also prove once and for all the superiority of the Aryan peoples over Jewish and Slav influences. A German victory would crush

international Marxism and international finance (the Jewish-Bolshevik conspiracy) and allow Germans to re-settle in the East.

Hitler's deepening engagement with foreign policy and *Raumfragen* (territorial issues) coincided with his growing interest in the *leitmotiv* of personality and his ideas of heroic leadership for Germany. Hitler argued that the state was the means of securing a victory over Jewish Bolshevism, but the state required the inspiration and guidance of an heroic leader-figure.

It was while he was in prison in Landsberg in 1924 for high treason after the abortive

> ### In Landsberg Hitler came to see himself as the future "great leader"

Munich Putsch, that Hitler came to see himself as the future "great leader". Prior to his imprisonment he had talked about messianic leadership but had seen himself merely as the "drummer" facilitating the way. As early as 1922, no doubt influenced by the example of Mussolini in Italy, Hitler began to stress the centrality of a Führer-figure as an integrating mechanism of the Nazi movement. Hitler had just emerged victorious from a power struggle of his own with his powers greatly enhanced. By 1921 it was clear that the Party was rapidly distancing itself from the original conception of Anton Drexler and members of the Party committee.

Hitler's attempts to turn the Party into a mass movement, his propaganda methods and his personal antipathy towards the "Drexler wing" came to a head in July 1921, when Drexler tried to recapture the direction of the Party, citing Hitler's "lust

Hitler with (from left to right) Emil Maurice, Christian Weber, Rudolf Hess and Hermann Kriebel. These men were among the first members of Hitler's bodyguard, and the Führer described them as his "first group of toughs".

An unemployed working class couple in Thuringia living in a self-constructed shack in the woods. The world economic depression of the late 1920s helped the Nazis, whose rhetoric provided easy answers to Germany's social problems.

for power and personal ambition" and his unwillingness to merge with other rival *völkisch* groups. Refusing to make concessions, Hitler resigned on 11 July demanding, as preconditions for his return, the retirement of the committee and dictatorial powers for himself. At extraordinary meetings on 26 and 29 July, Hitler was elected President of the Party with unlimited powers, forcing poor Anton Drexler into the political wilderness with the valedictory title of Honourary President. A few days later, on 3 August, the foundations of the SA (*Sturmabteilung* – Storm Troopers), the Party's paramilitary wing, were formed. (In

1933, Hitler would demand similar unlimited powers, eventually combining the roles of head of State, head of Government, head of Party and Supreme Commander in the unique title of Führer [Leader] of the German People.)

Having established his authority in the Party and reshaped its leadership structure, Hitler now decided to challenge the resolve of the Weimar Republic by mounting a Putsch in the Nazi stronghold of Bavaria. No doubt influenced by Mussolini's successful march on Rome in October 1922, Hitler decided to act. Taking advantage of Germany's hyper-inflation, the French and Belgian occupation of the Ruhr and government instability, Hitler, together with disaffected war hero General Ludendorff and local nationalist groups, sought to overthrow the Bavarian government in Munich and then march on "red" Berlin.

On the evening of 8 November 1923, Hitler mobilized units of the SA and burst into a public meeting at the Bürgerbräu-keller in Munich where the Bavarian state government under Gustav von Kahr was deciding whether or not to establish a

Sturmabteilung **(SA) – Storm Trooper – members on exercise outside Munich in 1923. Formed from ex-soldiers to provide protection for Nazi leaders at public meetings, the SA was later emasculated during the "Night of the Long Knives".**

separatist right-wing regime independent from alleged socialist influence in Berlin. Brandishing a gun, Hitler declared that he was forming a new provisional government. The next morning Hitler and Ludendorff marched through Munich at the head of 3000 men, only to be halted by police fire which left 16 Nazis and three police dead and brought the attempted Putsch (or more accurately, demonstration)

Freikorps **and Nazi Party members assembled in Munich during the Beer Hall Putsch – Hitler's ill-conceived attempt to take over the Bavarian state in November 1923. The Putsch was brought to a violent end by the Bavarian state police.**

to a humiliating and ignominious end. Hitler's plans had badly misfired. He was subsequently arrested and tried in an old Munich infantry school on 26 February 1924. The trial lasted for 24 days, and by the end of it Hitler had emerged as a national figure. He was accused of high treason and sentenced to only five years' imprisonment in Landsberg; the leniency of the minimum sentence reflected the right-wing nationalist sympathies of the judiciary. Hitler, who was not even a German citizen, had gained in confidence throughout the proceedings and at the end of the trial skillfully turned the tables on his accusers with an emotional propaganda speech.

> *Hitler was permitted to remain in Germany, but was banned from speaking in Bavaria*

Despite the severity of the crime, Hitler was released after only nine months, during which time he dictated the first volume of *Mein Kampf* to his loyal followers, Rudolf Hess and Emil Maurice. He was permitted to remain in Germany, but was banned from speaking in Bavaria and kept his head down during the year after his release, concentrating on writing volume two of *Mein Kampf*. By assuming full responsibility for the attempted overthrow of the Republic and refusing to make concessions to the authorities, Hitler transformed the débâcle of the failed Putsch into a personal triumph.

The failure of the Munich Putsch and his period of imprisonment elevated Hitler from an obscure provincial right-wing politician into a national figure, a symbol of implacable opposition to the Republic and the new figurehead of the *völkisch* movement.

With the re-establishment of the Party in February 1925, Hitler's position and status was greatly enhanced. Potential rivals such

A tense Hitler flanked by Alfred Rosenberg (left) and Dr Friedrich Weber of the *Oberland Freikorps* (right) during the Munich Putsch. Hitler was wounded during the affair – Rosenberg fled as soon as the shooting started.

as the North German *völkisch* leaders, Graefe and Reventlow, had broken away, disaffected, and drifted into other parties. The most serious challenge to his authority, however, came at the Party meeting in Bamberg in February 1926. In a five-hour speech Hitler headed off an attempt by the North German wing under Gregor Strasser (the second most powerful man in the

Party) to rewrite the Party programme along more "socialist" lines. By stressing his commitment to the 1920 programme and demanding loyalty to the Führer, Hitler outmanoeuvred his rivals and preserved the unity of the Party. Hitler's triumph was compounded by the capture of Goebbels, hitherto one of Strasser's strongest supporters. Writing in his diary in April

Rudolf Hess, who in World War I served in the same regiment as Hitler. A *Freikorps* member after the war, he joined the Nazi Party and took part in the Beer Hall Putsch. He later became Deputy Leader of the Party.

1926, Goebbels referred to Hitler as a "genius" and added: "Adolf Hitler, I love you." At the first Party congress to be held since the Putsch in July, the charismatic nature of Hitler's leadership and his claim to absolute authority were unanimously confirmed in a fanatical demonstration of Party unity.

The crisis was over. Having eliminated rivals from within the movement and reshaped its organizational structure in his own image, Hitler imposed his unimpeachable authority on the movement. When Otto Strasser, Gregor's younger brother, precipitated a similar challenge in 1930, Hitler's position and authority were unquestioned and Strasser was peremptorily dismissed from the Party. Hitler would experience a brief period of indecision following the death of his niece Geli Raubal in suspicious circumstances in 1931. But his personal obsession with power remained as strong as ever. Finally, in December 1932, Gregor Strasser resigned following a fundamental split over the primacy of the Party's original ideas set against unconditional faith in the Führer. On this occasion, Strasser's resignation did not lead to a split in the Party – or indeed to any form of factionalism. Hitler retained the loyalty of the movement. Henceforth, Hitler devoted much of his energy to reinvigorating Party cells and generally strengthening the Nazi Party nationally.

Hitler concentrated on the short-term goal of gaining power on a catch-all platform of national resurgence. To achieve this he decided to dismantle the organizational structure of the Party that his great rival Strasser had erected, and concentrate on seducing the electorate by means of propaganda. This required cynically disregarding many of the principles of the Party's 1920 programme – except those which constituted a means to power.

The period between the re-founding of the NSDAP in February 1925 and the *Reichstag* elections of July 1932, when the Nazis emerged as the largest political party in Germany (with 37.3 percent of the vote and 230 seats in the *Reichstag*), marks a sea-change in their fortunes. Nevertheless, it is important to remind ourselves just how insignificant Hitler and the NSDAP were to the centre stage of Weimar politics in the

> *Hitler concentrated on the short-term goal of gaining power on a catch-all platform*

period leading up to their electoral breakthrough. In the 1928 elections the Nazis polled only 2.6 percent of the vote (12 seats). Significantly, however, their activist base was growing in strength: it increased to more than 100,000 members. The onset of the World Depression in 1929, with its devastating effects on the German middle and working classes, helped win support for the Nazis. But equally, much of the success must be attributed to the creation of the "Führer-myth" and the quasi-religious identification of the movement with its leader, Adolf Hitler.

Nazi propaganda that depicted Adolf Hitler as an uncompromising opponent of the Weimar Republic had the effect of setting him apart from other politicians tainted by their association with the Weimar system, which had now become synonymous with political humiliation and total economic failure. Symbolic of the intensification of the cult of the leader was the compulsory "Heil Hitler" greeting for all Party members. The umbilical bond within

Hitler in Landsberg after the Putsch. He was found guilty of high treason in February 1924 and sentenced to five years' imprisonment. However, the trial provided him with his first opportunity to put his name on the national stage.

this "charismatic community" became so closely identified with the absolute authority of its leader that when Germans voted in elections in the 1930s, the ballot card referred not to the NSDAP but to the *Hitlerbewegung* (Hitler movement).

Behind the scenes, German establishment figures had also contributed to Hitler's rise to power. Although Hitler was fond of portraying himself as a man who had achieved greatness against the odds, from the early days of the Nazi Party in the 1920s elements of the German establishment actively helped Hitler. For instance, after the infamous Beer Hall Putsch in Munich in 1923, when the Nazis tried to seize power in Munich, Hitler was put on trial.

At his trial in February 1924, Hitler stood up and claimed full responsibility for the Putsch, which had cost the lives of three policemen. Before the judges at his trial, Hitler proclaimed: "Gentlemen, it is not you who pronounce judgement upon us, it is the eternal court of history which will make its pronouncement upon the charge which is brought against us [high treason] ... You may pronounce us guilty a thousand times, but the goddess who presides over the eternal court of history will with a smile tear in pieces the charge of the Public Prosecutor and the verdict of this court. For she acquits us."

Guilty of attempting a coup to topple the Weimar government, one would expect the German judiciary to hand down the severest penalty to the obscure Adolf Hitler. In addition, one would expect Hitler's arrogant behaviour at his trial to be met with a severe riposte from the angry judge. But in courting publicity, Hitler was not taking any real risk, for the judge who presided at his trial, Georg Neithardt, had sat on an earlier trial in 1922 where Hitler had been charged with violent affray. At that trial Neithardt had passed the minimum sentence possible of three months. Neithardt then wrote to the superior court asking that the three-month sentence be reduced to a fine. It was obvious that Neithardt was sympathetic to the Nazis. When Hitler made his courageous stand at his trial, he was, in fact, doing so in front of a sympathetic judge. Hitler knew he could say what he liked. While Hitler's behaviour before the court raised his profile across Germany, he knew full well that he was unlikely to be punished by the judge for his contempt of court, unlike those brought before the later Nazi People's Court.

Naturally, once in power in January 1933, the Nazis quickly tried to seize all the evidence of this trial. The Beer Hall Putsch proved that from the earliest days in the 1920s, elements within the German state, such as the judge Neithardt, gave tacit support to Hitler and the Nazis. This support would prove even more vital when, in the late 1920s, an economic downturn and an upsurge in support for the communists, drew the German upper classes to the Nazi Party.

CONTACTS WITH HIGH SOCIETY

Right from the beginning, in the 1920s, Hitler cultivated connections with the German establishment. These contacts would prove invaluable in the early 1930s when the Nazis seized power. In particular, Hugo Bruckmann, the wealthy Munich publisher, and Carl Bechstein, the piano manufacturer, provided an entry for Hitler into the highest echelons of German society.

Hitler's passage into high society was eased by the fact that both Frau Bruckmann and Frau Bechstein developed a motherly fondness for the charismatic Hitler. In 1923, Frau Bechstein even lent the Nazis her jewellery as surety against 60,000 Swiss francs that Hitler was able to borrow from a Berlin coffee merchant. It was also in the Bechstein mansion in Berlin that Hitler first met many of the senior German Army

> *This was a careful attempt to portray to the army a moderate side to the Nazis*

leaders and industrialists who would smooth his path to power.

Hitler cut an unlikely figure at these social gatherings. Unable to use his knife and fork correctly, people commented on his rough table manners. "He was never a gentleman, even later in evening dress," commented one *Freikorps* leader. Hitler, sporting a dog whip, would arrive wearing a gangster hat and a long trenchcoat over his dinner jacket. While this was novel attire for the well-kept salons of German high society, there was little doubting Hitler's charisma in drawing in Germany's social élite to the Nazi cause. Indeed, his eccentricity was part of the charm for wealthy Germans.

THE NAZIS AND THE ARMY

Hitler also targeted the German Army for Nazi infiltration. In March 1929, he made a speech appealing to the German Army to reconsider its commitment to the Nazis: "The future does not lie with the parties of destruction, but rather with the parties who carry in themselves the strength of the people, who are prepared and who wish to bind themselves to this Army in order to aid the Army someday in defending the interests of the people."

This was a careful attempt to portray to the army a moderate side to the Nazis. Then, a year later, three young German officers were put on trial for spreading Nazi propaganda within the German Army. The Nazis used the trial to draw the army closer to their cause. Put on trial in Leipzig, Nazi lawyers Hans Frank and Carl Sack represented the officers. Hitler appeared as a witness to assure the court that the Nazis had no intention of undermining the German Army. Many German officers sympathized with the Nazis, and were impressed by Hitler's argument that the Nazis only wished to seize power by constitutional means.

General Alfred Jodl later recalled that Hitler's Leipzig speech reassured the German Army that the Nazi leader was a man with whom it could do business. The Leipzig trial also showed, once again, the willingness of the German judiciary to give Hitler a propaganda platform. Hitler proclaimed at Leipzig that the German Army would again become a "great German people's army" that would determine Germany's future. The German officer corps listened to this message with interest. Senior German officers such as Hans von Seeckt and Ludwig Beck complained that the Leipzig trial should never have been allowed to proceed. When Hitler came to power in 1933, the German Army did nothing, seeing

Gregor Strasser. He led 300 men to Munich to support the Beer Hall Putsch, but they played no significant part in events. Afterwards, together with Ludendorff and Röhm, he organized a National Socialist Freedom Movement.

in Hitler a force for rearmament and restored prestige.

NAZIS AND INDUSTRIALISTS

As with the German Army, many German industrialists felt that they could use Hitler for their own ends. The Nazi Walter Funk, for example, acted as the go-between for German industrialists and the Nazis. The latter needed large sums of money to fight

Joseph Goebbels (left), originally Strasser's secretary, became a great admirer of Hitler during the Beer Hall Putsch. Goebbels was persuaded to make a public break from Strasser's radical group in 1926.

the elections and pay hundreds of full-time Nazi Party workers. The Nazis also needed money to pay for their private armies, the SA and SS, which by 1930 numbered more than

100,000 – a force larger than the German Army at the time. While the Nazis assiduously raised funds, the amount gathered was never enough. Therefore, German industrialists helped to provide the balance.

Who were the industrialists who bankrolled Hitler? There were men like Emil Kirdorf, the union-hating coal baron, who controlled a political slush fund for the Nazis called the Ruhr Treasury. German mining interests in the Ruhr supplied Kirdorf's fund with money in the hope that the Nazis would help smash the unions and the communists. An even earlier contributor was the steel magnate Fritz

> *While the Nazis assiduously raised funds, the amount gathered was never enough*

Thyssen who had met Hitler in 1923, after which he donated 100,000 gold marks to the nascent Nazi Party. With Thyssen there was Albert Voegler of the United Steel Works. These steel and coal magnates were a key source of funds for the Nazis in the crucial years of 1930–33 before Hitler came to power.

Other German industrialists provided tacit support: Georg von Schnitzler of the chemical giant I.G. Farben, August Rosterg and August Diehn of the potash industry, Cuno of the Hamburg-Amerika line, the Conti rubber interests, the Cologne industrialist Otto Wolf and the Cologne banker Baron Kurt von Schroeder. Many leading German banks and financial institutions also lent support: the *Deutsche Bank*, the *Commerz und Privat Bank*, the *Dresdener Bank*, the *Deutsche Kredit Gesellschaft* and

Germany's largest insurance concern, the *Allianz*. In his final drive for power, Hitler had considerable financial backing from the German business world. German business in the years 1930–33 provided the Nazis with millions of marks with which to pay for the day-to-day running of the Party and for election expenses.

THE ÉLITE AND HITLER'S RISE

Along with the judiciary, army officers and industrialists, the German conservative political élite also played a key role in the final run-up to Hitler being made Chancellor in January 1933. In late 1932 the Nazis were at a low ebb. Then, in January 1933, a turnaround in the fortunes of the Party came from an unexpected quarter: the former German Chancellor and aristocrat, Franz von Papen.

On 4 January 1933, Papen had a meeting with Hitler at the Cologne home of an intermediary, the wealthy banker Kurt Freiherr von Schroeder. Papen, seething over his treatment at the hands of the then Chancellor, Kurt von Schleicher, was willing to combine with Hitler to take power. In addition, Papen assured Hitler of the support of various wealthy Rhineland industrialists. Papen's subsequent account that he was not trying to undermine the Schleicher government at the January meeting with Hitler cannot be trusted. After all, why would Papen arrange a secret meeting behind Schleicher's back if the aim was to support Schleicher? It was the upper-class Papen who dragged the crisis-ridden Nazi Party back into a position from where it could take power.

The meeting at Schroeder's house began a series of talks between the conservative élite of Germany and Hitler, the erstwhile Viennese down-and-out and World War I corporal. This support from conservative politicians helped raise morale in the Nazi

Party. Hitler realized that if power was unattainable by way of the ballot box, it was a possibility through the back door of secret deals with high-ranking German conservative politicians.

Following the 4 January meeting, contrary to many accounts, money did not flood into the Nazi coffers from German industrialists. However, support from the German establishment was a great psycho-

> ## *By the middle of January 1933, Schleicher's position as Chancellor had deteriorated*

logical boost. The Nazis now felt that they had the political momentum to take them to the top. With this in mind, Hitler increased his efforts to win over the German populace. On 15 January 1933 there was a local election in the small agricultural state of Lippe. The Nazis saturated the local voters with propaganda. In the end, although the Nazis only gained a modest 4.8 percent increase in the vote, carefully prepared propaganda turned an insignificant gain into a Nazi triumph. Importantly, this result impressed President Paul von Hindenburg and the conservative élite. All the while, Hitler worked to exploit the differences between Papen and Schleicher, while simultaneously moving himself closer to the all-important Hindenburg.

By the middle of January 1933, Schleicher's position as Chancellor had deteriorated as agricultural interests, heavily infiltrated by the Nazis, condemned Schleicher's agricultural policies. Moved by these protests, Hindenburg began discussions with Hitler with the aim of creating a Hitler-

Geli Raubal (left), Hitler's niece and lover, with her mother, Angela Hitler Raubal. Hitler's increasing unreasonableness and jealousy led to her suicide in September 1931, an event that devastated the Nazi Party leader.

Papen administration. In the final meetings, Hitler negotiated with Hindenburg's son, Oskar, to arrange the new Nazi administration. It was no coincidence that, once the Nazis were in power, Oskar Hindenburg received a promotion from colonel to general along with thousands of acres of land.

When Schleicher protested to President Hindenburg about Hitler's talks with Hindenburg's son, Hindenburg did nothing. Schleicher's time as Chancellor was coming to an end. The last days of January 1933 were crucial as the German establishment tried to manipulate Hitler into a government that it could control. Hindenburg was worried about Hitler's impact on the German Army, and felt that if Hitler became leader a strong defence minister would be required to keep him under control. In all of this, Papen acted as Hitler's accomplice, helping to smooth the Nazi leader's contacts with those such as Hindenburg. For defence minister, Hindenburg chose Field Marshal Werner von Blomberg, without realizing that Blomberg was a strong Nazi sympathizer. Then, at the last minute, Hitler insisted on four major positions in the new government, besides the post of Chancellor for himself. Hitler got what he wanted and, on 30 January 1933, he was sworn in as the new German Chancellor.

While there were wealthy Germans, industrialists, political leaders, army leaders and police officers who opposed Hitler, too many influential members of the German establishment acquiesced, or actively conspired, to bring the Nazis to power. Hitler's triumph was not just a product of personal charisma, economic depression and the policies of the Nazi Party, but was possible because conservatives such as Schleicher, Papen and Hindenburg, along with self-interested industrialists, contrived to allow Hitler and the Nazis into power.

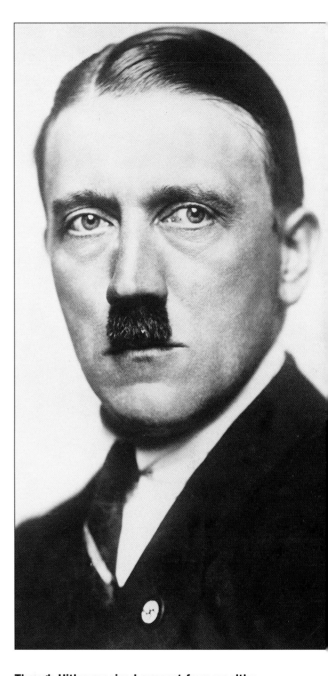

Though Hitler received support from wealthy industrialists and members of the German élite, his own resilience and self-belief, most notably after the Beer Hall Putsch, were also major factors in the Nazis' rise to power.

THE CONSOLIDATION OF POWER AND THE FÜHRER STATE

After Hitler had gained power in 1933, it became increasingly difficult for opposition groups to function, as the organs of the state and legal system became mere expressions of the Führer's will.

Hitler in Munich in the early 1930s. The Nazi state was a hierarchical structure, with the Führer at its apex. Hitler believed that the power of his will had brought him to power, and he grew increasingly to believe in its invincibility.

The 1928 elections brought to power the so-called Grand Coalition, consisting of the Social Democratic Party (SPD) together with a number of middle-class parties. Within two years this much-heralded

coalition that had been elected with such high expectations had collapsed, and Hitler would be asked to form a government. In January 1933, General Kurt von Schleicher's government, which had attempted to conciliate both Centre and Leftist interests within the Weimar system, was unable to secure a majority in the *Reichstag* and resigned. On 30 January, the President, Field Marshal Hindenburg, accepted a cabinet with Hitler as Chancellor, von Papen as Vice-Chancellor and nationalists, including Nazis, in other posts. Hitler owed his appointment as Chancellor not to the victory at a national

A mass Nazi rally at Nuremberg. Each rally was carefully stage-managed, with the use of speeches, flags, parades, marches and music all designed to increase support for Hitler and Nazism and to illustrate Nazi power.

election. Instead, in Alan Bullock's phrase, he was "jobbed into office by a backstairs intrigue". (see Chapter 1)

Nevertheless, despite the political machinations that took place within high politics prior to his appointment, Hitler became Chancellor constitutionally. The suggestion that Hitler and his Nazi Party somehow seized power is rather misleading. The Nazis

Paul von Hindenburg. A World War I hero, he was President of the Republic after the war. A natural conservative, he disliked Nazism. He once told the army commander, Hammerstein, that he would never bring Hitler to power.

fire of 27 February 1933 as a pretext for suspending civil liberties (the so-called "*Reichstag* Fire Decree") and conducting an election campaign (which had already begun) in circumstances highly favourable to themselves. In the elections of 5 March, the NSDAP made further gains, winning 288 seats but failing to secure an overall majority (43.9 percent).

There can be little doubt that the two most important ideas that distinguished the Nazis from other parties and allowed

> ## *By the time of his investiture as Chancellor, Hitler was the absolute autocrat of the Nazis*

the Nazi propaganda machine to mobilize widespread grievances were: the notion of *Volksgemeinschaft* (community of the people) based on the principle laid down in the Party programme of 1920 of *Gemeinnutz geht vor Eigennu* (common good before the good of the individual), and the myth of the "charismatic" Führer. The *Volksgemeinschaft* was to replace the divisive party system and the class barriers of the Weimar Republic and, in effect, offer the prospect of national unity without either a bloody revolution or the need to offer too many concessions to the working class.

The other element which appears to have been genuinely effective and unique was the projection of Hitler as a charismatic leader. The "Führer cult" had become synonymous with the NSDAP, and, from 1928 onwards, the panache of its propaganda in staging political rallies where Hitler could project his leadership and the faithful could give the impression

themselves are largely responsible for perpetuating this myth by continuing to refer to a *Kampfzeit* (period of struggle) and to their *Machtergreifung* (seizure of power). Having gained power, the Nazis used the *Reichstag* of being a dynamic movement, far exceeded those of other parties. The carefully constructed mass rallies with their marches, banners and flags, when combined with Hitler's histrionic speeches, provided Goebbels with the opportunity to synthesize the twin concepts of *Volksgemeinschaft* and the Führer cult in one political experience.

By the time of his investiture as Chancellor on 30 January 1933, Hitler was the absolute autocrat of the NSDAP. The state apparatus, with its formal lines of jurisdiction and hierarchies of authority, were unfamiliar and strange to him. He felt

The mass rallies at Nuremberg were part of a deliberate effort to increase the power of the Führer cult, whereby an encounter with Hitler (albeit at a distance) became an intense, almost religious event.

inhibited and insecure towards it. Moreover the traditional form of legally ordered, formally independent, juridically controlled state executive, represented constraints on his personal style of leadership. As the organizational form of the NSDAP had helped him secure victory and established his will as law within the movement, he simply transferred the independent position he held within the Party and its inner structure to the state. The gradual erosion of collective government was to be replaced by the absolute power of the charismatic leader. The "Party of the Führer" would now be extended to become the "Führer State". This was to have profound implications for the government of the Third Reich – and for those individuals and groups who opposed him.

CARROT AND STICK

Having gained power, Hitler had no intention of allowing the traditional ruling élite to regain control. He was determined to consolidate and extend his powers. A central feature of the so-called "Nazi Revolution" was Hitler's intention to restructure radically German society so that the prevailing class, religious and sectional loyalties would be replaced by a new heightened national awareness. In order to achieve this ambitious objective, the Nazi regime would have to manipulate large masses of people and attempt to move them to uniformity of opinion and action.

Hitler adopted a carrot and a stick approach. On the one hand membership of an exclusive, racial-*Völkisch* community was offered, while no opposition would be brooked from those unwilling to join, or from those deemed "undesirable". The pervasive fear of violence should not be underestimated, for it undoubtedly inhibited the forces of opposition. However, the menace of violence was, to some extent, counter-balanced by the positive image of new ethnic unity presented in the mass-media on an unprecedented scale.

In the years leading up to war – partly as an antidote to the increasing use of coercion and for the subsequent loss of liberty – propaganda eulogized the achievements of the regime. The press, radio, newsreels and film documentaries concentrated on the more prominent schemes: the impact of Nazi welfare services, "Strength Through Joy" (the Labour Front's agency for programmed leisure) and Winter Aid. Posters proclaimed the benefits of Socialism of the Deed, newsreels showed happy workers enjoying cruise holidays and visiting the People's Theatre for the first time, the radio bombarded the public's social conscience with charitable appeals,

> ## The intention was to move away from social confrontation

and the press stressed the value of belonging to a "national community" and the need for self-sacrifice in the interests of the state.

The intention was to move away from social confrontation towards conciliation and integration. Cheap theatre and cinema tickets, along with cheap radio sets and the cheap "People's Car", the *Volkswagen*, even the "People's Court" (*Volksgerichtshof*), were all intended to symbolize the achievements of the *Volksgemeinschaft*. The propaganda, therefore, presented an image of a society that had successfully manufactured

a national community by transcending social and class divisiveness.

The *Volksgemeinschaft* represented more than merely a cosmetic exercise, but it was never intended to embrace all Germans. The establishment of a socially and racially homogeneous *Volksgemeinschaft* excluded many individuals and groups on grounds of race, political affiliation and health. Jews, communists, social democrats, together with vagabonds, alcoholics and those with genetic diseases, were all deemed "outcasts" and

A solemn Hitler shakes hands with President von Hindenburg in 1934. Despite the fact that the elder statesman had said he would never bring the Austrian corporal to power, he was forced to swear in Hitler as Chancellor in January 1933.

excluded. Moreover, opposition was not simply discouraged, it was outlawed. In 1928, Hitler had told an audience that: "there is only one kind of law in this world and that lies in one's own strength." For Hitler, the law and the legal system were

Hitler at a ceremony to lay the foundation stone for the factory where the "People's Car" (in the foreground) would be constructed. This scheme was but one part of the Nazi effort to create the idea of a "People's Community".

simply a means to an end. To this end, Hitler's power after 1933 was greatly enhanced by his control of the instruments of the coercive apparatus of the state. Alan Bullock has perceptively noted: "Hitler never abandoned the cloak of legality; he recognized the enormous psychological value of having the law on his side. Instead he turned the law inside out and made illegality legal." The *Reichstag* fire of 27 February 1933 had provided Hitler with the pretext to begin consolidating the foundations of an authoritarian one-party state, and the "enabling laws" forced through the *Reichstag* beginning in March 1933 legalized intimidatory tactics and suspended civil rights in Germany.

The extraordinary "achievement" of the Nazis compared with other fascist and

Within 18 months of coming to power they had eliminated all forms of opposition

authoritarian regimes of the period was the speed with which they eliminated opposition. Within 18 months of coming to power they had erased all forms of political opposition by successfully preventing their opponents from organizing collectively. Within six months political opponents had been rounded up, incarcerated and outlawed. Within a year the quasi-autonomy of the regions had been crushed,

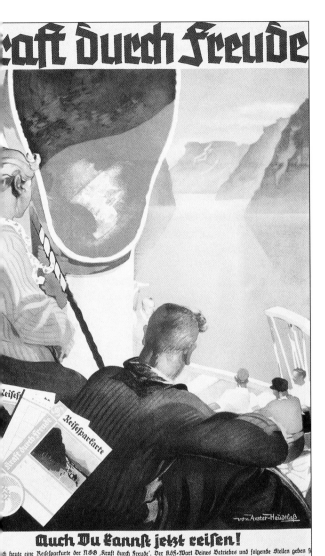

Yet another part of this plan was the Nazi "Strength Through Joy" (KdF) movement, which promoted the leisure and pleasure of German workers. This is a propaganda poster for the KdF Travel Pass.

and in June 1934 the potential threat posed from within the movement by Ernst Röhm and his SA had been brutally eliminated in the "Night of the Long Knives".

Ernst Röhm, a bullet-scarred, three-times wounded veteran of World War I, an *ex-Reichswehr* officer and local *Freikorps* leader, joined the fledgling and still tiny Nazi Party in its earliest days. Röhm, an experienced soldier and organizer of paramilitary forces, was the driving force behind the more muscular side of the NSDAP. In November 1921 he renamed the Party's sports and gymnastic division the SA (*Sturmabteilung* or Storm Troopers) and set about its reorganization and expansion. The SA under Röhm's leadership proved vital in the street battles that characterized much of German politics, and were the key to much of the Nazi Party's success in the late 1920s and 1930s.

HITLER AND RÖHM

While Hitler and Röhm were close – Röhm was one of the few among Hitler's close associates who addressed him using the familiar *du* (you) – there were tensions between the Party leadership and the SA. Hitler soon discovered that the SA was not entirely under his command. Although he was always received politely when he attended its meetings, parades and manoeuvres, it was clear that the members owed their primary loyalty to Röhm. Hitler was well aware that the organization was Röhm's private army, which often refused to take orders from Nazi Party officials. In an effort to mitigate this, Hitler established an élite bodyguard within the SA, which in 1925 became the *Schutzstaffel* (Defence Echelon, or more usually Protection Squad) – SS. The initially minuscule SS was made up of men upon whom Hitler could rely on totally.

Although nominally part of the SA, the relationship of the SS with its parent body was characterized by high tension and competition. The SA resented the élitism and intimate relationship between the SS and the Party leadership. Therefore, the SA leadership ensured that the SS often had to perform the more demeaning political tasks such as distributing Party literature and selling subscriptions to the Party newspaper. The SA ensured that the SS remained vastly smaller than its parent institution, and its membership declined from about 1000 to 280 by 1929. A series of old Nazi stalwarts struggled to protect the SS from SA interference, but the SS remained largely dominated by the SA.

On 6 January 1929 Hitler appointed 28-year-old Heinrich Himmler as head of the *Schutzstaffel*, with the title *Reichsführer der SS*. The SA leadership assumed that Himmler would be as easy to overawe as his predeces-

> ## Under Himmler the SS grew steadily; it reached 1000 members by 1930

sors. Himmler, however, was a man of great energy and drive and he devoted himself to expanding and reforming the SS.

Under Himmler the SS grew steadily; it reached 1000 members by 1930. A year later it had trebled. By contrast, SA membership increased to 170,000. The SA never had the same aspirations towards élite status in the manner of the SS; it was much more a mass movement. It also had many unruly elements, which resented much of the largely Bavarian NSDAP leadership. The Berlin SA rebelled against the appointment of Joseph Goebbels as Party *Gauleiter* (district leader), whose orders included the expulsion of anti-Hitler elements from the capital's NSDAP and SA organizations.

Despite the best efforts of Röhm, the rebellion spread throughout the north of

Germany. The SS remained totally loyal throughout the crisis, which eventually petered out through lack of financial support. In return, Hitler increased the responsibility of the SS, defining its role as

not just the *Elitetruppe* (élite troops) of the Nazi Party but also making it the movement's *Polizeidienst* (police service). This largely involved regulating the activities of the SA. This task often meant

Ernst Röhm (centre, looking skywards), the thuggish, homosexual and overweight SA leader and one-time friend of Hitler. His revolutionary ideas posed a threat to Hitler, and so he was eradicated during the "Night of the Long Knives".

searching the SA for concealed weapons, which added to the increasing bitterness between the two groups.

Himmler's reforms and reorganization ensured that the SS played a crucial role in Hitler's very rapid consolidation of power and elimination of his rivals both outside and inside the Party. On 27 February 1933, less than a month after the Nazi accession to power, the *Reichstag* building burnt to the ground. The Nazis used this as a pretext to clamp down on the communist opposition, dismantle the German constitution and

> ### The SA had always been the most "socialist" of the NSDAP's arms

institute a one-party state. Thus, with communist and parliamentary opposition gone, Hitler perceived that the main threat to Nazi rule came from inside the Party.

Even though the German Army was probably the one outside force that might be capable of overthrowing Nazi rule, it was unlikely to do so unless seriously provoked. However, the SA and its leaders seemed to be doing just that. By eliminating the threat that this organization posed, Hitler would also remove the one centre of power within the Nazi Party that remained outside his complete control.

The SA had always been the most "socialist" of the NSDAP's various arms

The continuing consolidation of power: Hitler celebrates the results of a plebiscite held three weeks after von Hindenburg's death which ratified the Führer's assumption of the double role of President and Chancellor.

and organizations. Indeed soon after the Nazi accession to power, Röhm was making speeches to massed rallies of the SA talking of the need for a "second revolution" and claiming that: "The National Socialist struggle has been a Socialist Revolution. It has been a revolution of the workers' movement. Those who made this revolution must be the ones to speak up for it." Such talk was a considerable embarrassment for Hitler, who had assiduously courted Germany's financiers, industrialists and landowners in his bid for power. This was another point of contention, as many in the

The body of President von Hindenburg lying in state at his country house in Neudeck, Prussia, guarded by *Reichswehr* soldiers in August 1934. His death removed a brake, albeit small, on Hitler's increasing power.

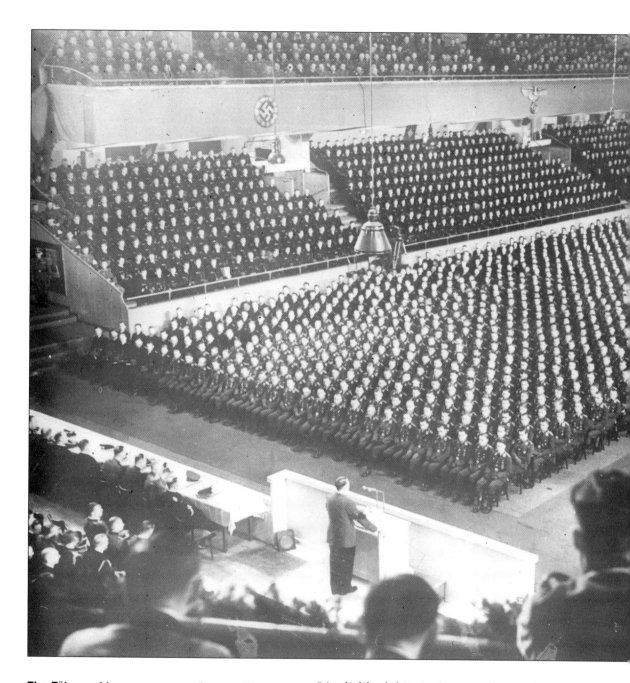

The Führer addresses a group of army officer cadets in Berlin. There is no doubt that Nazi rearmament proved popular among the *Wehrmacht* (armed forces), and thus ensured the military's support for the regime.

SA disliked his intimate relationship with such groups. Hitler could not fail to be embarrassed by such rhetoric.

The most serious point of contention, however, was Röhm's military ambitions

perhaps more than any other if his aspirations for a Greater Germany were to come to fruition. In the short term if Chancellor Hitler wanted to ensure that he succeeded the ailing President Paul von Hindenburg as Head of State, he needed the backing of the members of the German officer corps. But the latter were becoming increasingly anxious in the face of Röhm's explicit military ambitions for the SA.

Military support was not unquestioning, though. This is General Ludwig Beck, Chief of the General Staff. He opposed Hitler's expansionist foreign policy and resigned following the invasion of Czechoslovakia in September 1938.

for the SA. Hitler ideally wanted to retain Röhm's support, but the SA leader's attitude towards the army forced Hitler to choose between his friend and the institution whose loyalty he required

Röhm demanded that his SA gain a prominent role within Germany's armed forces, and he himself had aspirations to command the *Reichswehr*. In February 1934, he claimed that the SA was the true army of National Socialism and that the regular army should limit itself to training duties. He also said that the Ministry of Defence should be reorganized, the implication being that he should be at its head.

Understandably, the German military leadership was alarmed by such talk. The thought of admitting Röhm's unruly street fighters into the army en masse horrified it,

> ## Röhm – a notorious homosexual with a weakness for young males

and the possibility of being commanded by Röhm himself, a notorious homosexual with a weakness for young males – as he said himself: "I am an immature and wicked man" – with limited regular military experience, was beyond contemplation. As General von Brauchitsch, at the time a divisional commander in Prussia, recalled: "Rearmament was too serious and difficult a business to permit the participation of peculators, drunkards and homosexuals."

THE POWER OF THE SA

Hitler's response was to tell Röhm that this role for the SA was out of the question, and instructed him that the SA would be limited to training under the army's supervision. The army was delighted and, while Röhm fumed, the Defence Minster, General Blomberg, demonstrated its loyalty to Hitler by dismissing all non-Aryans and adding the Nazi eagle and swastika to German military uniforms, thus politicizing an erstwhile non-political organization.

Yet the SA remained a potent force in German politics. Röhm's SA was 4.5 million strong; the *Reichswehr* – limited by the World War I peace settlement – contained a mere 100,000 men. Hitler also knew that such a large organization remained important to the Party and that some sort of resolution was required. He first tried to reason with his old friend, telling Röhm that he ought to: "Forget the idea of a Second Revolution. Believe me, don't cause any trouble." As a safeguard, Hilter sent all 4.5 million SA men on leave throughout June 1934.

Quite apart from the threat the SA posed to the Nazi Party, the one man who would profit most from the demise in the influence of Röhm was the SS *Reichsführer* Heinrich Himmler. The SS, now about 80,000 strong, remained part of the SA, but Himmler craved independence. However, he maintained some feelings for his superior and old comrade Röhm, and therefore he passed on the task of undermining the SA to his deputy, Reinhard Heydrich.

Heydrich at once began to spread rumours of SA plots to seize power and collected and fabricated documents to support this. Although Hitler was probably inclined to settle the problem once and for all, Himmler and Heydrich did their utmost to force him into a decisive decision. The two SS men provided Hitler with plenty of "evidence" of SA misbehaviour and, more seriously, a forthcoming SA uprising in Berlin. Eventually he was convinced and declared: "I've had enough. I shall make an example of them." On 28 June 1934 he ordered the elimination of the SA leadership.

Two days later Hitler himself, with a number of SS men from the *Leibstandarte*,

Adolf Hitler's SS guard unit commanded by Sepp Dietrich, arrested Röhm and much of the SA leadership at Bad Weissee. Meanwhile, back in Berlin, the rest of the *Leibstandarte,* supported by the newly formed concentration camp guard detachments under the ruthless Theodor Eicke, rounded up SA men and other rivals. Eicke was entrusted with the task of dealing with Röhm. Hitler decided, some time during 1 July, to have the SA leader killed. Himmler, as a chief organizer of the purge, telephoned Eicke, who was by now at the SS offices in Munich, and told him to go and kill Röhm, who was being held in Munich's Stadelheim prison. Eicke, accompanied by two SS officers, shot Röhm dead his cell after he refused the option of committing suicide.

Estimates of the number who were murdered during the purge vary. Hitler admitted to 77 victims in a speech to the *Reichstag* on 13 July 1934, yet historians set the figure anywhere between 100 and 1000. Whatever the case it broke the power of the SA forever. The organization was reduced from 4.5 million to just over one million and it was stripped of its weapons. The SA never regained the influence it had once held.

In contrast, Himmler and the SS profited immensely from the purge. On 26 July 1934 the *Völkische Beobachter* (*Nationalist Observer*) announced that "in consideration of [its] very meritorious service" the SS was elevated to the "standing of an independent organization within the NSDAP". Himmler had finally gained his autonomy, and his organization's ascendancy within Nazi Germany was ensured. Himmler, who had held the title of *Reichsführer*-SS for five years, was now just that. Finally, he was directly subordinate only to Hitler. Also, contrary to Hitler's earlier promise to the

The *Reichstag* on fire during the evening of 27 February 1933. The next day President Hindenburg suspended all civil liberties in an emergency decree, which became constitutional law in March – Germany became a police state.

army that it and the navy would be the only armed organizations in Germany, he gave the SS permission to form armed units.

The "Night of Long Knives", as the purge of Röhm and the SA was popularly known, showed something of the nature of Nazi

Goebbels (fifth from left), Göring (fifth from left) and Hitler (fifth from right) inspect the damage caused by the fire at the *Reichstag*. A feeble-minded Dutchman, Marius van der Lubbe, was convicted of starting the fire, and executed.

rule. Hitler had turned against one of the most important Nazi institutions, the SA, a formidable paramilitary force of some 4.5 million men led by one of his closest and oldest allies, Ernst Röhm, and to do so he had used another Nazi organization, one that would profit most from the SA's destruction – the SS – to bring Röhm's force down. Although he was initially reluctant to turn against his friend, Hitler did this because he needed the army more than an SA as envisaged by Röhm. The German generals were overwhelmingly grateful and responded by giving Hitler a remarkable

hierarchy. On the "Night of Long Knives", Himmler and the SS proved that they were both the fittest and most ruthless. For individuals and groups that remained, a process of *Gleichschaltung* (coordination), by which all political, economic and cultural activities were assimilated within the state, ensured that a sufficient degree of conformity would sustain the regime in power until 1945. In practice this meant that all political parties, trade unions, youth organizations and churches were either dissolved or brought under state and Party control. The final constitutional check on Hitler's dictatorial position disappeared when the 87-year-old President Hindenburg died in August 1934 and Adolf Hitler assumed the office of Head of State as well as that of Chancellor.

A PLIANT PEOPLE

Repression and fear generated during the first 18 months in office, together with the dissolution of independent organizations that had previously acted as buffers between the individual and the state, partially explain the quiescence of the German population. The Nazi regime repressed its potential enemies with systematic thoroughness and brutality. Between 1933 and 1939, for example, 12,000 Germans were convicted of high treason. And a total of 40,000 Germans had fled the country for political reasons.

During the war, when the number of offences punishable by death rose from three to 46, a further 15,000 were condemned to death. It has been estimated, for example, that 30,000 members of the German Communist Party (KPD) were murdered by the Nazis and a further 300,000 sent to concentration camps. It is estimated that more than 2000 working class members of illegal resistance organizations in the Rhine-Ruhr area alone lost their lives to Nazi terror.

level of loyalty over the next 11 years. As for the SS, which carried out the task with consummate efficiency, Himmler and his men were rewarded commensurately, gaining a position of almost unparalleled power in Nazi society.

Hitler believed very strongly in Social Darwinism, that in the struggle for survival only the fittest would survive, and he was quite willing to apply this to the Nazi

The apogee of centralized power: Hitler at Nuremberg in September 1938. By this time he was dictator of Germany, had re-occupied the Rhineland, occupied Austria and the Sudetenland of Czechoslovakia.

Of course, there was dissent (mainly the result of rifts that existed before 1933), but this occurs in one form or another in any political system during such a prolonged period in power. Such "opposition" as existed in Nazi Germany remained isolated and was largely confined to grumblings about material conditions. While accepting that dictatorship gradually corrupts the moral fibre of its citizens and that resistance became increasingly difficult as the Nazi State consolidated its authority, one is nevertheless left with the legitimate question: why was there so little resistance, particularly at the beginning?

The reasons for the lack of coordinated protest are many and complex. Suffice to say that it is difficult to conceive, particularly after the death of President Hindenburg, of individuals or organizations being able to mount effectively a challenge to Hitler or impose constraints on the increasing radicalization of Hitler's programmes. A small group of generals led by Ludwig Beck opposed Hitler's foreign policy in the late 1930s, but were undermined by France's and Britain's decision to appease Hitler over Czechoslovakia. The advent of World War II in 1939 made resistance even more difficult. In wartime any form of dissident behaviour can be construed as violating the patriotic duty of allegiance owed to one's country. Not surprisingly, the number of treasonable offences increased – as did the sentences that were handed out during the war. The image of an ordered and disciplined society, strongly led and united behind Hitler, is the image that the Nazi propaganda machine wished to convey.

Hitler did not, however, silence all opposition. There remained individuals and groups who were willing to conspire against the regime, at great danger to themselves. Few, tragically, were able to escape the clutches of the Third Reich's security forces and many paid with their lives. It is to these brave "conspirators" that I would now like to turn my attention.

Reich Party Day in Berlin in 1938: phalanx after phalanx of storm troopers march through the streets cheered by the masses. The strength and power of Nazism can be appreciated by comparing this image with the one on page 15.

GERMAN INTELLECTUAL AND LEFT-WING RESISTANCE TO HITLER

Many Germans were appalled by the reality of the Nazi State, with its terror tactics on the streets, arbitrary arrests and disregard for civil liberties in general, but resistance was a dangerous affair.

Once in power, Hitler acted ruthlessly. He had two chief objectives: first, to remove anyone in the old German establishment and even in the Nazi hierarchy (both had conspired against him prior to 1933) who

The memorial inscription at Neuengamme concentration camp near Hamburg. Many of those German opponents to Hitler, whose activities are described in this chapter, met their deaths in this particular camp.

might threaten his power; second, to create a wholly centralized state. Hitler made the major decisions but his chosen representatives had enormous self-centred leeway to achieve them. Hitler did not, however, silence all his opposition.

His opponents were drawn from a wide range of political, social and religious groups. They tended to be motivated by a combination of personal, religious and ethical principles. According to Peter Hoffmann, one of the leading authorities, "the relation between National Socialism and the Resistance is a key to comprehending the Nazi system."

Gestapo headquarters in Prum. The Gestapo was the secret police of the Third Reich, and had informers throughout Germany. As such, it made it both difficult and dangerous for individuals to organize anti-Hitler movements.

Individuals and groups who were not prepared to accept National Socialism unconditionally could respond in a variety of different ways. These responses ranged from complete passivity to active conspiracy. There has been considerable debate in recent years as to how these various forms can best be described. Therefore before attempting to evaluate German resistance (or conspiracies) in the Third Reich, first we need to distinguish what we mean by "resistance". We can start with the historians' debate about how the word resistance or "opposition" should be used. How narrowly or broadly should historians define resistance activity? Originally it was applied solely to highly motivated political activists who became organized to overthrow the Third Reich. In recent years historians have focused on three aspects of opposition: the scale of the active opposition, the credit for the resistance to the Nazis and the motivation for opposition.

FORMS OF RESISTANCE

What constituted resistance in Germany? Some historians, notably Ian Kershaw, have proposed the following distinctions:

> *Resistance* Active participation in organized attempts to work against the regime with the conscious aim of undermining it or planning for the moment of its demise.
>
> *Opposition* A wider concept comprising many forms of action with partial and limited aims, not directed against Nazism as a system and in fact sometimes stemming from individuals or groups broadly sympathetic towards the regime and its ideology.
>
> *Dissent* The voicing of attitudes, frequently spontaneous and often unrelated to any intended action, which in any way whatsoever ran counter to or were critical of Nazism.

Kershaw, I. *Popular Opinion and Political Dissent in the Third Reich*, pp.2–4.

By distinguishing opposition and dissent from resistance, one can separate organized from spontaneous activity, and actions directed against the Third Reich as a whole

from those with more limited aims. It is also possible to talk of more general acts of non-conformist behaviour that were not intended fundamentally to challenge the regime but represented individual acts of infringement of the norms of the state. Detlev Peukert, for example, sketched a pyramidal model building from a broad base of "non-conformity" (much of it private), through "refusal of cooperation" (*Verweigerung*), to

Women collectors for the "Winter Aid" programme meet Hitler on the "Day of National Solidarity" in 1937. Even a refusal to contribute to this massive charity for the relief of the poor could bring threats of violence.

"protest", to, finally, the narrow peak of "resistance" proper (*Widerstand*), which was restricted to forms of behaviour "in which the National Socialist regime in its entirety was rejected".

By emphasising the impact of the Nazi regime on all areas of everyday life (grass-roots behaviour), a multi-faceted picture of spheres of conflict between rulers and ruled has emerged that has shifted our perception away from the traditional totalitarian model of a monolithic police state that completely eradicated opposition activity. On the gamut of dissident behaviour, non-conformism might

Willy Brandt, a member of the *Sozialistische Arbeiterpartei Deutschland*. He left Germany in 1933, took Norwegian citizenship and then fled to Sweden following the German invasion in 1940. He later became Chancellor of West Germany.

include a parent's refusal to send a daughter or son to the Hitler Youth in contravention of repeated official injunctions; or the refusal of a worker to return the appropriate Hitler salute when greeted by a Party member. Dissident behaviour might also include listening to enemy broadcasts in violation of radio

> ### *Resistance to Hitler and the Nazi regime can be divided into three broad categories*

guidelines or offences against the Malicious Gossip Law of 20 December 1934. Such offences were viewed and prosecuted by the National Socialists as acts of resistance.

More far-reaching, in that it represented one stage further in the wholesale rejection of the regime, was protest, though this might still represent a single issue, such as the Bishop of Münster's campaign against euthanasia.

Finally, there is the fundamental, principled and total resistance to Nazism with no other aim than to bring about the regime's overthrow. It is in this latter category that one would place the more famous conspiracies to remove Hitler from power. The benchmark here is whether such behaviour was significant enough to worry the police authorities, whether individuals spoke out publicly against aspects of policy, and, finally, whether the regime was rejected as a whole. In other words, what effect did an individual or group behaviour and action have on the regime?

Fritz Rehn, a German lawyer appointed by Hitler to be President of the People's Court in Berlin. This was one of a number of special Nazi courts established to try political offences; the one in Berlin was charged with trials of high treason.

The investigation of the grass-roots behaviour of the German population under Nazism led to an interesting conclusion that, dependent on particular social circumstances, not everyone could realistically organize to overthrow the regime – or indeed plot meaningfully against the police state. Thus while, for example, members of the government and military élites, such as General Ludwig Beck and Count Helmuth von Moltke, did have the expertise and opportunity to overthrow the regime, it is hard to imagine how an ordinary worker could have undertaken anything directly comparable. Resistance to Hitler and the Nazi regime can therefore be divided into three broad categories: political, religious and military. Within these broad categories I shall be analyzing resistance that took place within the labour movement, the middle class, the churches, among German youth and within the German armed forces.

OPPOSITION IMPOTENCE

The most obvious question is why the other political parties failed to take effective action to stop the rise of the Nazis as long as legal action was still possible. There can be no unequivocal answer to this question. Unquestionably the political parties failed to recognize the need to unite against the threat from the fascist Right and continued their disastrous policy of non-cooperation that played into the hands of the Nazis and facilitated their consolidation of power. This applied particularly to the Social Democrats (SPD) and the Communists (KPD), who were more sharply opposed to each other

Arvid Harnack, a co-leader of one of the most important communist resistance groups in Germany, the Red Orchestra – *Rote Kapelle* – a name given to the group by the Gestapo, which was formed in 1935.

The other leader of the Red Orchestra was Harro Schulze-Boysen, shown below. He was brutally tortured by the Gestapo following his capture, and both he and Harnack were executed at Plötzensee in December 1942.

than they were to the Nazis. Therefore, a more substantive explanation for this political failure to resist Nazism must be sought within the complicated political and economic history of the Weimar Republic. In other words, the internecine conflict on the Left and what one writer has referred to as the enthusiasm of the conservative Right to act as grave-diggers to the Republic.

Once the Nazis gained power and swiftly eradicated political parties, it was hardly realistic for an individual to undertake acts of political resistance under such an oppressive and all-embracing totalitarian police state. For individuals who opposed the regime, one of the few options was passive resistance in the form of a refusal to cooperate. These acts of considerable individual courage consisted of a refusal to contribute to a Nazi fund-raising campaign such as Winter Help (much of which found its way into arms production), or the refusal to greet other citizens with a "Heil Hitler" salute or to display the swastika flag on official occasions.

The ultimate individual act of non-conformity was suicide. Such acts of

rassing to a government that claimed popular appeal, did not, however, represent a threat to the regime's existence.

Emigration was another form of non-cooperation. About 400,000 individuals left Germany between 1933 and 1939, of whom 35–40,000 left for political reasons, the remainder being Jewish. The Central Committee of the SPD moved to Prague in

Communist leader Ernst Thälmann (left). The _Reichstag_ fire was used by the Nazis as an excuse to arrest him and other communists. He was held in various concentration camps, until finally shot at Buchenwald in 1944.

> ### *Thirteen of the 213 names on the list of victims after the plot committed suicide*

desperation were largely in anticipation of ill-treatment. One example was Jochen Klepper, son of a Protestant pastor, who committed suicide together with his Jewish wife and step-daughter in December 1942. Not only had he been deprived of his livelihood, but his step-daughter and wife were likely to be deported to a death camp. Thirteen of the 213 names on the list of victims after the 20 July 1944 plot committed suicide. Although the number of suicides did increase marginally in the first few years of the regime, by 1942–43 they actually fell below suicide rates in the late 1920s. All these are examples of individuals following their conscience but cannot be construed as resistance. Such individuals neither intended nor did they have the opportunity to weaken the regime or overthrow it. Individual acts such as these, while they may have proved mildly embar-

May 1933, then to Paris in May 1938 and finally to England in 1940. The KPD Committee moved to Paris in 1933, then Prague, then back to Paris in 1936 and finally to Moscow in 1939.

As we have seen, one of the major aims of the Nazi state was to eliminate organized political opposition. Within six months of coming to power political opponents had been rounded up, incarcerated and outlawed. The speed with which political opposition was emasculated forced those that remained to organize underground activities such as clandestine printing operations producing leaflets aimed at maintaining contacts and establishing new ones.

> ## *An estimated 1000 socialist and communist groups were active between 1935 and 1936*

In the early years of the regime such spontaneous opposition on the part of members of the persecuted political opposition was more concerned with survival and preserving the spirit of resistance. Common to most of the individuals who joined resistance groups was a moral objection to the way in which the Nazis persecuted all those who refused to subscribe to their beliefs. As such, the spontaneous opposition groups that emerged in the years 1933 and 1934 were made up of individuals from all walks of life and from all levels of German society. If a group is defined as consisting of two or more members, an estimated 1000 socialist and communist groups were active between 1935 and 1936, according to Nazi police records.

Most of these underground groups were eventually discovered by the Gestapo. The Nazis made a point of weeding out social democrats from the police, the civil service and the armed forces. In 1936, for example, more than 11,500 people are known to have been arrested for illegally undertaking clandestine activities for the SPD. In 1937, the estimated figure was just over 8000, and by this time SPD leaflets were being collected at a rate of 4000 a month.

Although the SPD and KPD were declared political opponents of the Nazis, it is also undeniable that many from within their ranks were not. Many former socialists and particularly communists joined the Nazi ranks, attracted by its combination of National Socialist ideas and regeneration – exchanging one form of totalitarian dogma for another.

Underground political activities were made all the more dangerous by the Nazi practice of installing *Blockleiters* in every local community. These "men of confidence" were ubiquitous and would operate in blocks of flats, housing estates and so on, informing the authorities of any non-conformist or suspicious behaviour. Despite (or perhaps because of) the Nazis' success in eradicating political opposition, underground work actually increased during the first years of the Nazi regime. As the German socialist and communist movements were being infiltrated and destroyed, conspiratorial work had to be learned and this could only be undertaken in small organized groups.

WALTER LOEWENHEIM

Two such groups were the *Neu-Beginnen* (the New Beginning) and *Der Roter Stozstrupp* (the Red Assault Party). *Neu-Beginnen* was founded in 1929 by Walter Loewenheim, who was then working under the pseudonym "Miles". The son of a Jewish merchant family, Loewenheim had originally been a member of the German Communist

Youth Organization (KJVD) and the German Communist Party. In 1927, he had broken with the KPD and in 1929 had joined the German Socialist Party, believing it to represent a more fertile political organization for his ideas. *Neu-Beginnen* was a non-partisan group made up largely of disaffected young communists and social democrats and included men such as Fritz Erler, Richard Löwenthal and Waldemar von Knoerringen.

Initially they were concerned with the failure of Weimar party leaders to unite the two mutually hostile left-wing parties. Members of the group were encouraged to work as opposition cells within the KPD and SPD, and this proved excellent training for their later underground resistance work. When the Nazis came to power in 1933,

Walther Ulbricht, a founding member of the German Communist Party, escaped from Germany to Paris in 1933, later returned to Germany in 1945 in the wake of the Red Army, and thereafter headed the East German government.

Neu-Beginnen continued as before, building up cadres that, it was hoped, would act as catalysts for the creation of a mass movement of opposition to Nazism, and would be in a position to help with recon-struction in Germany after the Nazi collapse. In August 1933, Loewenheim published a manifesto, *Neu-Beginnen*, which gave the group its name. The manifesto was published by Graphia

Rudolf Hess addresses workers in the Machine Hall of the AEG works in Berlin. Despite the support of industry for the Nazis, groups such as the Red Orchestra were able to establish cells among the workers of companies such as AEG.

publication caused an enormous stir, having been smuggled into Germany in large number because it corresponded to the mood and plans of German socialists and, moreover, offered a theoretical response to the practical necessities of underground activity. In the manifesto, Walter Loewenheim attributed the

> *It was hoped that a mass movement of opposition to Nazism would develop*

success of the Nazis to the Left's lack of unity and called for a popular front to come together to oppose fascism and bring about a social revolution.

Although its main centres were in Berlin and the Ruhr, it proved successful in establishing a network of cadres across Central Europe, including branches in Czechoslovakia, Austria, Switzerland and Spain. A central committee called the "Circle" was at the top; its members were the brothers Walter and Ernst Loewenheim, Eberhard and Wolfgang Iskow (the latter had been a former *Reichswehr* officer and member of the KPD's military or counterintelligence apparatus), as well as Walter Dupré and Frank Schleiter. One must also mention Edith Schumann and Vera Franke, who assumed key roles within the organization.

In 1934, the SPD's executive in exile cut off financial support and the group around Loewenheim broke with the party. A dejected

Publishing House, the publisher of the exiled German Social Democratic Party's executive committee in Czechoslovakia. It bore the subtitle, *Fascism or Socialism: Basis for Discussion among Germany's Socialists*. The from foreign radio broadcasts and newspapers smuggled in from abroad. The group was particularly active in 1936–37, when activists were able to send details of Hitler's preparations for war to the SPD in exile. In 1937 *Neu-Beginnen* joined forces with the "Popular Front Group", made up of former SPD and trade union officials, and produced with them a series of publications outlining a strategy for overcoming National Socialism.

The most important result of this cooperation was an extension of the Popular Front's 10-point programme, culminating in a

> ## *Further arrests in the autumn of 1938 brought Popular Front activity to an end*

revised manifesto under the title *German Freedom*. Further arrests in the autumn of 1938 brought its activity inside Germany virtually to an end, and many of the top officials were sentenced to long prison terms. Löwenthal and von Knoerringen were forced into exile and developed close links with groups such as the *Internationaler Sozialistischer Kampfbund* (International Socialist Battle League) and the *Sozialistische Arbeiterpartei Deutschland* (German Socialist Workers' Party), which included among its ranks a young Willy Brandt. All these individuals were to play a prominent role in the SPD after 1945.

The non-partisan underground group *Der Roter Stozstrupp* (The Red Assault Troop) was led by the journalist Rudolf Küstermeier. This group was set up in Berlin in 1933 and consisted of young blue-collar workers, white-collar workers and students. The group attempted to bring together individuals

Workers heat steel rods at the Borsig Locomotive Works in Berlin. The clandestine Red Assault Party found recruits among such blue-collar workers, but resistance groups were prey to infiltration by the Gestapo.

Loewenheim emigrated in 1935, despairing of achieving anything in National Socialist Germany, but his work was continued by Erler, von Knoerringen and Löwenthal. Its main source of propaganda was a leaflet entitled *Das Greune Otto* (*The Green Otto*), which specialized in up-to-date news taken within the German Left and maintain an engagement with representative politics in the face of Nazi repression and political arrests.

One of the objectives of *Der Roter Stozstrupp* was to collect and distribute information that had been either suppressed or falsified by the National Socialist government. It published a paper under the title *Der Roter Stozstrupp*, which was printed from various homes in Berlin. In the summer of 1933 it had a circulation of 200–250 and a decentralized distribution network that sent the paper to most regions of the Reich, where its contents were fully or partially reprinted. However, it suffered like most small groups working underground in that it relied on trust and secrecy, but was eventually infiltrated and disbanded by the Gestapo.

The work of such groups tended to be the same throughout Germany. Anti-Nazi material was either published clandestinely or was smuggled in from the outside and distributed. These groups also acted as a means of refuge for victims of political persecution. The resistance collected money to support the families of political prisoners, or alternatively they provided false passports to help them escape from political tyranny. Foremost in this respect was an organization known as "Red Aid", which set about

The research laboratories at AEG in Berlin. Infiltration of the industrial workforce by German resistance groups was small-scale and largely ineffective, not least due to the benefits reaped by the workforce from Nazi economic policies.

removing Nazi propaganda and replacing it with its own defiant slogans. Anti-government leaflet campaigns were another tactic. Left-of-centre groups consisting predominantly of communists, but including trade unionists and social democrats, such as the Saefkow-Jacob Group, targeted sections of the population with their propaganda literature. One flyer produced by Saefkow-Jacob, the *Soldier's Letters*, was directed specifically at members of the *Wehrmacht*.

Because of their generally defensive forms of activity, these socialist groups proved more difficult to penetrate than comparable communist underground groups. The possibility of their access to and distribution of printed materials, which were invariably provided by Sopade, formed their core activity. In 1936, the Gestapo estimated that 1,643,000 leaflets had been distributed illegally. In the main, most of the propaganda material was distributed to known and reliable connections and was not publicly disseminated. Having rejected mass agitation as suicidal, the SPD was mostly concerned with information and enlightenment.

The heyday of the more agitational socialist cells was 1934; hardly any resistance groups in the classic sense of the term survive the following year. Almost without exception they fell victim to the Gestapo's close surveillance and were convicted by the People's Court, sometimes in huge public "show trials" involving dozens or hundreds of defendants. Some groups, such as the Markwitz Circle, made up of social democrats, carried out acts of sabotage. All these conspiratorial activities were undertaken under the constant threat of imprisonment, incarceration in concentration camps or being sentenced to death for high treason. While these individual and spontaneous acts of resistance were unquestionably courageous and proved irritating to

the Nazi authorities, they remained too isolated to be truly effective.

The German Communist Party (KPD) had become the third largest party in the final years of the Weimar Republic. At the end of 1932, the KPD had approximately 360,000 registered members. As a section of *Comintern* (Communist International), the party had

> *There remained an implacable belief in a strong, disciplined German workers' movement*

pursued an ultra-leftist policy since 1929. It had also recognized the dangers in a situation in Germany that was resembling a civil war. Thus, the leadership had prepared for a period in which the party would be banned and for the requisite underground activity. In fact, party leaders on various levels, and from precinct to local chapter, had been rehearsing for the actual event since the end of the 1920s. However, there remained an implacable belief in a strong, disciplined German workers' movement, which was admired throughout the world as a vanguard of proletarian solidarity. Thus the party was caught off-guard by the speed and brutality of the Nazi assault on its rank-and-file membership and the imprisonment of its charismatic leader, Ernst Thälmann.

Nevertheless, the KPD agreed with the social democrats, the trade unions and the bourgeois parties that Hitler, like his predecessors, would be in power for only a short period of time. The Nazis, on the other hand, acted decisively; 17 of 28 communist regional leaders were arrested, together with at least one-third of the 81 *Reichstag* deputies and 63 Prussian state representatives who had been elected on 5 March 1933. At the beginning of July, Fritz Heckert, the German representative of *Comintern*, had to acknowledge that the party had already lost substantial parts of its mid-level functionaries during the first weeks of March. He estimated that approximately 11,000 communists had been arrested (this figure proved subsequently to be a low estimation). Forced into action by the coordinated speed of the Nazi attack, the *Politburo* decided to set up three of its members – Wilhelm Pieck, Franz Dahlem and Wilhelm Florin – in Paris to oversee tasks that could no longer be dealt with in Germany. The remaining four members – Walther Ulbricht, John Schehr, Hermann Schubert and Fritz Schulte – remained in Berlin to manage matters as best they could.

The political struggle was waged primarily with propagandistic writings, referred to as "propaganda as a weapon". Flyers about current affairs, small-format newspapers continuing in the style of outlawed local, regional and national newspapers, factory newspapers and leaflets were produced and distributed under the greatest danger and on constantly changing underground printing presses. *Die Rote Fahne* (*The Red Banner*), the party's newspaper, continued to be printed until 1935. Isolated actions such as chanting in the backyards of houses in Berlin, hoisting red communist banners on buildings, cutting the main electrical cable at one of Hitler's speeches (as occurred in Stuttgart), and secret May Day celebrations, were activities supposed to attest to the party's survival and strength of will to hold out. Increasing amounts of prohibited literature revealing the horrors of everyday life under National Socialism were smuggled over borders, and "dissident" literature, such as the eyewitness report *Mörderkager Dachau*

An *Illustrierter Beobachter* (*Illustrated Observer*) article on Dachau concentration camp, December 1936. Such publications reinforced the image of the Nazis as guardians of the state against subversive elements of society.

(*Murderers' Camp Dachau*) and the Brown book about the *Reichstag* fire, came back into Germany disguised as works by Schiller and Goethe.

Revealingly, the KPD never seriously coordinated an armed uprising, despite repeated Nazi news reports about discoveries of communist weapons caches. Even though underground propaganda doubtlessly strengthened group identity and communist solidarity, it did not bring down Hitler and the Nazis. Gradually, under the particular conditions of the Third Reich, an

The fate of many German anti-Hitler group members: hard labour in a concentration camp. These inmates at Dachau are carrying out heavy construction work. The average survival time of a prisoner in a work camp was nine months.

Comintern leadership during late 1934, and resulted in an official strategic and tactical change of course at the Seventh World Congress of the Communist International in August 1935. Recognizing its weakness, the *Comintern* suddenly offered an alliance to groups it had previously denounced.

A new popular front policy signalled a pragmatic readiness to work with socialist and bourgeois-democratic forces in all countries that were either threatened by, or already ruled by, fascism. This had important implications for German resistance. In implementing this new policy, the German Party Conference that followed near Moscow (codenamed the Brussels Conference), consisting largely of German emigrants with only a few delegates from the German underground, agreed to revise the old centrist organizational structure in favour of smaller independent groups. In future such underground resistance groups would make their own decisions about the manner and extent of their activity.

THE RED ORCHESTRA

One of the most important communist resistance groups was the *Rote Kapelle* (Red Orchestra), a name given to it by the Gestapo. The group was formed in 1935 and the two leading figures were Harro Schulze-Boysen and Arvid Harnack. It managed to infiltrate cells in large firms such as AEG, Shell and Borsig, and it was particularly active in Berlin, where it infiltrated the German Post Office and the German National Railways with its agents.

Schulze-Boysen was born in 1909, the son of a naval officer who was a nephew of Admiral von Tirpitz. His mother, Marie Louise Boysen, was a friend of Göring's. In 1932–33 he worked for an anti-Nazi periodical called *Gegner* (*Opponent*), and regularly took part in communist street fights against the Nazi Brownshirts. Schulze-Boysen formed part of a loose-knit group of

irreconcilable contradiction emerged between the dissemination of propaganda and more open forms of agitation. Having witnessed its youth, military and sports organizations crushed, a process of rethinking began to emerge within the "drawing-room communists" whose sympathies were communist (although they were not paid-up party members), made up largely of artists and literary figures. He was arrested by the Nazis in 1933 and sent to a concentration camp, where he was subjected to brutal physical interrogation.

When he was released, thanks to his mother's influence, he joined the German Air Force that had been secretly rearming since the Nazis came to power, having been banned under the Treaty of Versailles (1919). In 1936 he married Libertas Haas-Heye, who was the granddaughter of the Kaiser's favourite, Philipp Count zu Eulenburg. It was Göring, in fact, who

> ## *Schulze-Boysen established other important links with like-minded individuals*

helped find him a job in the Press Section of the new "official" Nazi Air Ministry. From 1936 onwards he was actively engaged in producing and distributing anti-Nazi leaflets. Some of these leaflets, including information on Nazi air force strategy in the Spanish Civil War, were sent to the Russian Trade Delegation. As a result he aroused the interest of Russian Intelligence.

In 1939 Schulze-Boysen was put in touch with another communist sympathizer, Arvid Harnack, who worked in the American section of the Ministry of Economics and who had married a Jewish-American student, Mildred Fish. Schulze-Boysen remained the dominant figure within the group, and it was his unconventional individualism and dash which guaranteed that the *Rote Kapelle* never became a fully fledged communist cell obediently receiving and carrying out orders

from Moscow (unlike, for example, the Knöchel Organization under the leadership of Wilhelm Knöchel, the only leading KPD cadre to succeed in illegitimately returning to Nazi Germany).

A particular intellectual and artistic milieu set the tenor for loose forms of meetings and communications that got along largely without rigid organization or covert rules. Schulze-Boysen was not the type of man who would take orders from anyone. By 1939, he had managed to get himself transferred to the Attaché Group in the Air Ministry, which was responsible for all reports sent by air attachés in German missions abroad. He managed to pass these reports to Moscow via the Russian Trade Delegation, which had provided him with three wireless transmitters. The radio network that was established furnished the Soviets with numerous reports on the political, military and economic situation, particularly arms production.

Schulze-Boysen established many other important links with like-minded individuals working in governmental departments. These included Horst Heilmann in the Foreign Broadcasts Monitoring Service, and Countess Erika von Brockdorff and Frau Schumacher in the Ministry of Labour. Between July 1941 and the autumn of 1942 the *Rote Kapelle* produced an underground newspaper, *Die Innere Front* (*The Inner Front*) once (sometimes twice) a month, with a circulation of approximately 600 copies. He also ran another clandestine printing operation, *Der Vortrupp* (*The Vanguard*). Both publications appeared in various languages and were also directed at members of the conscripted foreign workforce. Speeches by Bishops Galen and Wurm, Churchill, Stalin, Thomas Mann and Ernst Wiechert were distributed with the aim of strengthening intellectual resistance. The group also attempted to counter Nazi anti-Soviet propaganda, such as

Admiral Wilhelm Franz Canaris, head of the _Abwehr_, the German military intelligence organization. He became an anti-Nazi and was implicated in the July 1944 Bomb Plot. Found guilty of treason, he was hanged in April 1945.

the exhibition entitled "Soviet Paradise" in the spring of 1942, by daubing anti-Nazi posters that drew attention to political repression and economic hardships in Germany. After 1939, contacts were strength-ened through Wilhelm Guddorf and John Sieg, former editors of _Die Rote Fahne_, with cells of the communist resistance in Berlin and Hamburg that were operating independently of the party leadership in Moscow. By 1942, the _Rote Kapelle_ had become an important source of information to the Soviet Union and a considerable irritant to the Gestapo. Indeed, Admiral Canaris (Director of the Counterintelligence Office – _Abwehr_) claimed that the organization had been responsible for the lives of 200,000 German soldiers. By this time, Schulze-Boysen was working on large-scale plans to sabotage and paralyze German armaments industries.

The _Rote Kapelle_ conspiracy was uncovered by chance. The group's weak link had always been its communications with Moscow. There was only one operator for the three or four radio transmitters and he was inadequately trained. A Russian agent who had parachuted into Germany in August 1942 to facilitate communications was caught by Admiral Canaris' _Abwehr_ and turned over to the Gestapo. Under torture he provided information making it possible to eliminate most of the organization.

On 30 August 1942, Schulze-Boysen was arrested and subjected to the most brutal torture. With the communists, whom they regarded as the worst of all enemies of their country, the Gestapo was utterly merciless. Schulze-Boysen was eventually executed on 20 December, having apparently died bravely. Sadly his wife, Libertas, was induced to reveal numerous names. A total of 118 arrests were made and about 55 people, including 19 women, were executed, being slowly strangled to death by a rope hung from a hook. A further 50 were sentenced and executed after a second farcical trial in December. On specific orders from Hitler, Mildred Harnack and Erika von Brockdorff were also executed, even though they had only been given prison sentences.

According to Terence Prittie (1964) the *Rote Kapelle* was probably the best-organized, large-scale spy network in Nazi Germany. With its collapse, communist resistance became increasingly concentrated on two rather unusual types of organization. The first was in the concentration camps, the second among prisoners-of-war in the Soviet Union. There has been considerable controversy as to whether Schulze-Boysen and his comrades were heroes or traitors. Some historians have suggested that as members of the *Rote Kapelle* and other communist groups, they supplied the Russians with military information, and *ipso*

> **The Gestapo managed to break up the Uhrig-Romer Group in Berlin and Munich**

facto they were traitors who should not be mentioned in the same breath as other resistance figures such as von Stauffenberg, Beck, Leber and others. Schulze-Boysen's activities included both propaganda and espionage. Both were intended to bring about the collapse of National Socialism and this, he believed, could only be achieved by defeating Germany in war. It is a familiar story of ends justifying the means.

One other group that warrants a mention in the context of communist resistance is the so-called Saefkow-Jacob Group. This group was led by a trained machine builder, Anton Saefkow, and was one of the largest communist resistance organizations in wartime Germany. Shortly before the beginning of the war in 1939, Saefkow, who had been a functionary of the KPD during the Weimar Republic, was suddenly released by the Nazis from a concentration camp

where he had been incarcerated since 1933. Having gathered a small group of communist sympathizers, he began to develop links with the communist *Uhrig* (watch-like) resistance groups around 1941. However, the Gestapo managed to break up the Uhrig-Romer Group in Berlin and Munich in February 1942. When the Gestapo also infiltrated the communist resistance group around Bernhard Bästlein and Franz Jacob in Hamburg in October 1942, Jacob, a former representative in the Hamburg city government, escaped to Berlin and made contact with Anton Saefkow.

UNDERGROUND CELLS

By the beginning of 1943, Saefkow and Jacob began to mobilize members of the Berlin KPD cells who had managed to escape the Gestapo's clutches. They established a new network of underground cells, mainly factories linked to the armaments sector. Once again, militant tactics were rejected in favour of sabotaging armaments production and passive work attitudes. The Saefkow-Jacob Group was well-organized, with a rigid division of labour that set out areas of responsibility for those producing flyers, false documents, security and so on. More importantly, the Saefkow-Jacob Group sought constructive contacts with other communist resistance groups in Thuringia, Saxony and Anhalt, such as the Schumann Group and the Neubauer Group.

As a result of these links and the common goal of resistance against National Socialism, a new KPD leadership emerged in the autumn of 1943 which referred to itself as the National Committee "Free Germany" (NKFD). In accordance with the NKFD's goals, all anti-fascist groups were to be mobilized in a broad resistance movement. From now on, the Saefkow-Jacob Group often signed its flyers, in which the group demanded an end to the war, the overthrow of Hitler, and a democratic Germany with the "NKFD – Berlin Committee".

Saefkow-Jacob also made determined efforts to establish links with other resistance groups, including members of the social democrats and bourgeois resistance. Discussion had been initiated between his group and social democrats Julius Leber and Adolf Reichwein, both members of the Kreisau Circle (see Chapter 4). Bernhard Bästlein also joined up with the group towards the end of the war. Bästlein's communist cells operated in the dockyards and metal processing factories of Hamburg and northwestern Germany from 1940 until his arrest in March 1942. He managed to escape from prison after an Allied bombing raid on Hamburg and immediately went underground. He was eventually re-arrested but resurfaced to join the Saefkow-Jacob Group, having escaped from the Berlin-Plötzensee prison after a bombing raid on 30 January 1944.

By this time the group had increased its conspiratorial propaganda against Hitler by acquiring a press, and this greatly increased the production of anti-Nazi propaganda flyers. It also facilitated the production of the *Soldier's Letters* directed specifically at members of the *Wehrmacht*. In addition, Saefkow-Jacob helped establish small NKFD groups in *Wehrmacht* support organizations in Berlin, such as in the Office of Army Clothing and Accessories.

THE GESTAPO CLOSES IN

By the beginning of 1944 the Gestapo was closing in on the Hamburg cells. From January until October 1944, there were around 14 trials involving members of the communist resistance movement; at least 22 death sentences were handed down, including that against Robert Abshagen, one of the principal members of the Bästlein Group. In all, more than 70

members of the organization lost their lives. The last ones were murdered on 21 and 23 April 1945, in Neuengamme concentration camp. All hope of developing a coordinated resistance against Hitler was severely undermined by this wave of arrests. Discussion between the Saefkow-Jacob Group and Leber and Reichwein of the Kreisau Circle could not, as a result, be intensified. The Saefkow-Jacob Group was now everywhere in retreat.

> *More than 60 members of the group were murdered before Hitler was finally toppled*

Bästlein was arrested on 30 May 1944; Jacob, Saefkow and many collaborators in the struggle were arrested on 4 July. The People's Court sentenced Saefkow, Jacob and Bästlein to death on 5 September 1944. The sentences was carried out on 18 September, in Brandenburg-Görden prison. More than 60 members of the group were murdered before Hitler was finally toppled.

Communist attempts to eliminate Hitler's regime from within were severely weakened by the success of the Gestapo in infiltrating first the Bästlein Group, then the Knöchel Organization and finally the Saefkow-Jacob Group. Because of its broad activities the communist underground provided the most leads for the Gestapo, and thus almost inevitably suffered from the highest number of informants than any other resistance movement. Social democratic opposition, on the other hand, managed to hold itself together only for a limited time. While it is true that brave individuals emerged from within the socialist and communist ranks to risk their lives in conspiratorial activities against Nazism, it is also true that no major, towering figure dominates the leftists' landscape with the sole intention of eliminating Hitler.

Statistics published by the Gestapo provide an idea of the extent of underground conspiracy activities. In February 1935, for example, 12 resistance groups with a total of 6105 members were uncovered. In the course of 1935, the Gestapo discovered 5067 distribution points for underground literature. A total of 612 of the texts were new to the Gestapo. Reports to Berlin show that 1599 members of the left-wing opposition were arrested for engaging in illegal socialist activities. In 1937, the figure had risen to 8058 with 17,168 trials for "political treason". Although the Gestapo successfully infiltrated resistance groups, the arrests did not destroy the spirit of resistance. In 1941, the number of individuals arrested for illegal communist and social democratic activities (11,405) remained nearly the same as in 1935.

The ready mixed concrete section at Neuengamme concentration camp. Members of the communist Bästlein Group, captured after an intensive Gestapo operation, were murdered here on 21 and 23 April 1945.

RESISTANCE AND THE MIDDLE CLASS

Though Nazism appealed to large sections of the German middle class, there were intellectuals who were alarmed at the realities of Nazi rule, and began to plot the overthrow of the Third Reich.

There are a number of reasons that explain why the National Socialists were able to gain a great deal of support in nationalist and Christian sections of the middle class. Three of the most important factors include:

Hitler at a youth rally in the Berlin Olympic Stadium, 1938. Many middle class Germans equated the Nazis with stability and economic prosperity at home and success abroad, and thus readily gave their support to the regime.

• The Nazi's skilful use of "nationalist" propaganda, which kept alive and stirred up hatred of the Allied nations that had won the war in 1918. By perpetuating the "stab-in-the-back" myth, the Nazis systematically maligned democratic politicians allegedly responsible for the consequences of military defeat and promised, at the same time, to tear up the Treaty of Versailles, restore Germany's national pride and lead it back to military greatness/glory.

• Because of their total hostility towards everything "Marxist" or "Bolshevist", which the middle class perceived as the major threat to their traditional hierarchical position in German society.

• Because of the Nazis' intellectual provincialism, which was incensed at the "general corruption of morals" that was allegedly encouraged under the conditions of "decadence and materialism" that conservatives associated with the Weimar Republic.

MIDDLE CLASS OPPOSITION

For these reasons, the bourgeois middle class was even less suited to organized resistance than the forces of the political Left. Broadly, middle class opposition manifested itself in the form of individuals or groups formed spontaneously for motives based on moral objections to dictatorship (rather than ideological principles). Many of these individuals would hold strong religious beliefs, and so a further characteristic of middle class opposition was its links to different religious denominations and church groups. Through the experience of living under National Socialism, a loose mosaic of middle class (or bourgeois) opposition consisting of individuals and groups, often overlapping, developed over a period of time. One of the interesting features of middle class opposition was that due to a shared moral repulsion their

Intellectuals and liberals were disturbed by the rhetoric of leading Nazis. Hermann Göring, for example, President of the *Reichstag* from 1932, had stated: "It's not my business to do justice; it's my business to annihilate and exterminate."

interests often overlapped. This coalescence of what one might refer to as the "other Germany" was composed of a mixed assortment of high officials, diplomats, trade unionists, academics and scientists, many of

Hans Frank, the head of the Nazi Association of Lawyers and of the Academy of German Law. Among his pronouncements was that "love of the Führer has become a concept in law". He was hanged after World War II as a war criminal.

the norms of a constitutional state that had existed before January 1933.

While in theory the Weimar Constitution was never abrogated, Hitler's position as Führer and exclusive representative of the nation's will was quickly consolidated. In order to achieve this position of unrestricted power, the Nazi state intimidated a judiciary which sanctioned what was happening, and by its total subservience to the "will of the Führer" removed its traditional function as an independent third force of the state. Although few changes were made to civil law, the Nazis proved ruthlessly opportunistic in utilizing the criminal law for their own ends. By gradually subverting legal norms to executive SS-police action acting under the guise of "Führer-power", the Nazis could rely on the compliance of a national-conservative judiciary that had remained essentially hostile to the liberal principles of the Weimar Republic (which had protected individual rights against excesses of the state). Therefore, without necessarily being staunch Nazis, many judges and lawyers welcomed the Nazi regime in 1933 for its promise to restore a more authoritarian notion of "law and order" and, by implication, the status of the judiciary.

FRANZ GÜRTNER

Led by Reich Minister of Justice, Franz Gürtner (who was not a Nazi), the erosion of legality began shortly after the *Reichstag* fire, when the "Decree for the Protection of the People and the State" (passed on 29 March 1933) retrospectively imposed the death penalty on van der Lubbe for allegedly setting fire to the *Reichstag*, even though the death penalty for arson had not existed at the time of the offence. In fact the "*Reichstag* Fire Decree" (as it was popularly known) was used indiscriminately to arrest any political opponent of Nazism who could

whom held and continued to hold important positions within the National Socialist system. Despite their different backgrounds, they agreed on a series of goals. Many reacted angrily to the regime's increasingly criminal methods, and demanded a return to now be interned without trial. Whereas 268 cases were tried for high treason in 1932, in 1933 the figure had risen to over 11,000. In March 1933, in order to deal with treason trials resulting from the "Lex van der Lubbe", a new system of Special Courts, operating without juries, was introduced. It was Gürtner who also gave legal sanction to the massacre of the SA leadership in June

> ### *The People's Court denied defendants most of their rights, including that of appeal*

1934 ("Night of the Long Knives") by claiming that the state had "anticipated" treasonable action, and that the measures were justified on the grounds of "self-defence". The progressive erosion of the rule of law and the old *Rechtstaat* was further continued by the setting up in April 1934 of the so-called "People's Court" (*Volksgerichtshof*) to deal with cases of treason. Many Party purists hoped that the People's Court would become the direct expression of a *völkisch* concept of the law. Staffed by five judges, only two of whom needed to be lawyers, and using juries made up only of Party officials, the People's Court denied defendants most of their rights, including that of appeal against a verdict. By 1937, however, the People's Court found itself increasingly supplanted by the massive expansion in the power of the merged police and SS, who were operating outside the conventional framework of the law as a direct executive organ of the "Führer's will".

The basis for the interpretation of all laws was now the National Socialist philosophy, as expressed in the Party programme, the

Franz Gürtner was Hitler's Minister of Justice from 1933 until his death in 1941. Responsible for dismantling the old system of German justice and the creation of Nazi courts, he was actually a conservative rather than a rabid Nazi.

speeches of the Führer and "healthy popular feelings". Carl Schmidt, a constitutional lawyer, defined the principles of Nazi law as simply "a spontaneous emanation of the Führer's will". This view was made quite explicit in a speech made by Hans Frank, the head of the Nazi Association of Lawyers and of the Academy of German Law, in 1938:

"1. At the head of the Reich stands the leader of the NSDAP as the leader of the German Reich for life.

"2. He is, on the strength of being leader of the NSDAP, leader and Chancellor of the Reich. As such he embodies simultaneously, as Head of State, supreme State power and, as chief of the Government, the central functions of the whole Reich administration. He is Head of State and chief of the Government in one person. He is Commander-in-Chief of all the armed forces of the Reich.

"3. The Führer and Reich Chancellor is the constituent delegate of the German people, who without regard for formal preconditions decides the outward form of the Reich, its structure and general policy.

"4. The Führer is supreme judge of the nation ... There is no position in the area of constitutional law in the Third Reich independent of this elemental will of the Führer.

"The Führer is not backed by constitutional clauses, but by outstanding achieve-

One manifestation of German law being nothing more than the Führer's will: the destruction of a synagogue during *Kristallnacht* on 9/10 November 1938. Two days earlier Hitler had stated: "In Germany the Jew cannot hold out."

ments which are based on the combination of a calling and of his devotion to the people ... Whether the Führer governs according to a formal written Constitution is not a legal question ... The legal question is only whether through his activity the Führer guarantees the existence of his people." (Welch, 2000: 46–7)

Thus Hitler's position of absolute power was justified not in legal-rational terms as Chancellor and Head of State but in charismatic terms as Führer of the German *Volk* – not a state, but a German nation as a racially determined entity. As the custodian of the nation's will, constitutional limitations could not be imposed on his authority. The legal system and individual judges had no right to question the decisions of the Führer, which were increasingly disguised as laws or decrees, and thus given the facade of "normality". Such "normality" could, however, be violated at any time by individuals or organizations, for example the Gestapo, who could claim to be operating within the sphere of "Führer-power". In this way the constitutional state was delivered into the hands of the "healthy feelings of the nation" which, it was claimed, would generate the strength and energy necessary for national revival and Germany's quest to become a dominant world power.

KRISTALLNACHT

One example of this move away from constitutional norms was the *Kristallnacht* (Crystal Night) in November 1938: nation-wide pogroms resulting in the murder of 91 Jews, the injuring or maltreatment of countless others, the burning of 191 synagogues, the arbitrary destruction and looting of 7500 Jewish shops and other property, and the arrest and imprisonment in concentration camps of around 30,000 male Jews. Legislation during the following few days

forced Jews out of the economy and onto the fringes of society. Almost 80,000 Jews were forced to leave Germany in 1939, compared to around 40,000 in 1938 and 23,000 in 1937.

The *Kristallnacht* in particular served as a rallying point for these "other Germans". On the one hand they rejected a return to the

> ### 80,000 Jews were forced to leave Germany in 1939, compared to 40,000 in 1938

liberal parliamentary system of the Weimar Republic, whose deficiencies, in their view, had facilitated Hitler's rise to power. For the future Germany, they perceived a "third way" between Western capitalistic individualism and Eastern European socialistic collectivism. They continued to think primarily in terms of the state, even though some within the resistance began to widen their horizons to embrace European cooperation as the only means of reconstruction after the devastation of World War II.

Typical of this type of national-conservative conspirators was the Wednesday Club/Society in Berlin. This was a small group of largely intellectuals who met regularly for an informal exchange of views. The group included prominent names such as the philosopher Sprenger, the surgeon Sauerbruch, the lawyer Carl Langbehn (who acted for *Reichsführer-SS* Himmler), former ambassador Ulrich von Hassell and the Prussian Minister of Finance Johannes Popitz. In 1938, after the *Kristallnacht*, the conservative but anti-Nazi Popitz offered his resignation as Finance Minister of Prussia, only to have it refused. The group would splinter into a number of different

A man clears away the broken glass from the Jewish Bedding Establishment the morning after *Kristallnacht*. To pay for the state-sanctioned destruction, Germany's Jews were fined and Jewish businesses and property were confiscated.

"personas". For example, it was sometimes referred to as "The Establishment" due to the fact that it was made up of older and more mature figures, most of whom had at one time assumed positions of responsibility. When General Ludwig Beck, former Chief of the German General Staff, joined he rapidly became the centre of attraction. In March 1942 the Berlin conspirators agreed to

formally acknowledge Beck as their leader and coordinator. In June Beck had addressed the Club on "The Lessons of Total War". The discussions that took place within the group were characterized by a high level of intellectual and critical quality.

This group did not, however, plot subversive action aimed at overthrowing the Third Reich. Rather, it acted as a sort of "political colloquium" questioning the existing political system and discussing alternative forms of government with possible ways of overthrowing Hitler. It was more concerned with thinking about the form of government that might replace

> *The programme sought to reform Germany in the spirit of the Prussian reform period*

National Socialism once it had been overthrown or destroyed. Through Popitz, who attempted to influence Himmler against Hitler, the group developed connections to Carl Friedrich Goerdeler, the civilian driving force of the 20 July Group and the Kreisau Circle associated with von Moltke.

In 1941 Beck and Goerdeler drew up a memorandum, based on earlier drafts. Called *The Goal (Das Ziel)*, it stressed the need to place responsibility on the individual, while at the same time giving him as much freedom as possible. The programme sought to reform Germany in the spirit of the Prussian reform period of the nineteenth century: there was a strong emphasis on self-government and the dominant position of the Reich Chancellor. On the one hand, Germany was to have a strong central government with a parliament whose power was limited to setting the budget; the plan also envisaged extensive self-government at the regional level. *The Goal* was fashioned by and large by Goerdeler's views, and only rarely were the ideas of third parties allowed to penetrate. One exception to this rule was the plan concerning the German Trade Union, which was composed at the behest of Wilhelm Leuschner, the former deputy chairman of the General German Federation of Labour. But it coincided with Goerdeler's scheme to transfer to the trade unions large segments of the social security system, in particular the unemployment insurance system.

Hassell, the former German Ambassador in Rome, had earlier drafted a plan for a new government based on a return to liberty, justice, the rule of law and respect for human life and for minorities. Hassell's plan anticipated a return to the old 1914 Reich borders. A further splinter group consisting of Popitz, his former pupil Jens Peter Jessen (Army General Staff), Erwin Plank (former

A wrecked Jewish-owned shop in Berlin after *Kristallnacht*. It is estimated that 7500 Jewish shops and other properties were destroyed, while around 30,000 male Jews were arrested and imprisoned in concentrations camps.

State Secretary in the Reich Chancellery), Langbehn and von Hassell, drew up in 1942 a draft Basic Law that would have transformed the structure of Germany into a unitary state similar to the French model. Within this preliminary constitution the *Wehrmacht* would remain a prominent institution, although all Reich ministers and officials would be removed. The Nazi Party, the Gestapo and the concentration camps were to be dissolved, and laws discriminating against Jews were to be suspended "pending a definitive disposition".

TERROR IN COURT

Next to *The Fundamental Principles for the New Order* by the Kreisau Circle (see page 91), *The Goal* is perhaps the most important constitutional plan published by the resistance. Nevertheless, the political Left viewed the group that drew up the programme as reactionary and conservative, referring to them dismissively as the "grey-haired government", and feared that they were concerned more with restoring the old status quo than destroying National Socialism. This was probably an undeserved epithet, for Popitz, von Hassell, Langbehn and Jessen were all executed after the failed assassination attempt on Hitler's life in July 1944.

Another right-of-centre group consisting primarily of economists was the so-called "Freiburg School". This group included Constantin von Dietze, Alexander Rüstow, Leonhard Miksch, Walter Eucken, Wilhelm Röpke and Alfred Müller-Armack, although they embraced members outside of economics. A working committee under the chairmanship of the distinguished historian Professor Gerhard Ritter drafted a memorandum entitled *Political Social Order: An Attempt at Reflection by the Christian Conscience in Our Difficult Times.* Part of the memorandum, which Goerdeler

helped formulate, fell into the hands of the Gestapo in 1944, leading to the arrest of Ritter and others who had collaborated. Through Pastor Dietrich Bonhöffer, who was murdered in the Flossenbürg concentration camp in April 1944, there had been contact between the Freiburg group and the Confessional Church. They did not develop close links with the military conspiracy and none of them lost their lives.

Three resistance groups that existed parallel to, but independent of, one another in Freiburg are referred to as the "Freiburg Circles": the Freiburg Council, the Bonhöffer Circle and the Erwin von Beckerath Task Force. While members of the Freiburg Circles were not immediate members of the circle of conspirators involved in the 20 July 1944 assassination attempt on Hitler, they maintained contacts especially with Goerdeler and Popitz. Some of them, such as von Dietze, Eucken, Lampe and Günter Schmölders, were consulted as experts on economic questions by the Kreisau Circle. Indeed, their economic ideas

> *The political Left referred to the group as the "grey-haired government"*

were accorded a place in the plans of the resistance groups involved in the 20 July group. Their neo-liberal theory anticipated a state "sponsored" competitive system as a middle path between laissez-faire liberalism and a centrally planned economy. Within such a system, the benevolent state would bring about meaningful economic competition by making it impossible for particular interests to control the market.

The economists' involvement in the Freiburg Circles was a result not only of having taught together at the university, but also of their membership of the Confessional Church. On Adolf Lampe's initiative, the Freiburg Council was formed at the end of 1938 for the purpose of discussing unresolved theological questions in a free exchange of ideas. The discussion group met regularly under the stewardship of the distinguished historian Gerhard Ritter until 1944. In a brief minute, Ritter summarized the conclusion of the discussions about how engaged Christians should respond to a government that openly disregarded Christian values and God's commandments. Largely due to von Dietze's connections with leading members of the Confessional Church

Prussian Minister of Finance Johannes Popitz (front row, second from right) on trial for his life after the July 1944 Bomb Plot. Popitz was a member of the Wednesday Club/Society, a group of middle class anti-Hitler intellectuals.

in Berlin, a smaller working group emerged from the ranks of the Freiburg Council at the end of 1942. This was the Freiburg Bonhöffer Circle. This closely knit circle was supposed to work out principles for a new order in Germany. The memorandum was intended to serve as a discussion paper at a world conference of churches after the war. The core group, consisting of Ritter, von Dietze, Eucken and Lampe, produced the main part of the pamphlet *Political System of the Community*. Towards the final stages of the draft, Carl Goerdeler and others were brought in to the discussion. After the 20 July Bomb Plot, the pamphlet fell into the hands of the Gestapo, which led to the arrest of von Dietze, Lampe and Ritter.

Their arrest brought to an end the work of the third Freiburg Circle, the Erwin von Beckerath Task Force, whose members were largely made up of economists. In addition to von Dietze, Eucken and Lampe, there was also Erwin von Beckerath, Gerhard Albrecht, Erich Preiser, Günter Schmölders, Heinrich von Stackelberg and Theodor Wessels, as well as Franz Böhm, Clemens Bauer and Fritz Hauenstein. His group was formed in 1943 out of a committee of the Academy of German Law that had been

> ## The planned final report was never published because of the arrest of the Freiburgers

suspended by the Nazi regime at the start of the war, but had continued its work privately. The Task Force set about writing a number of mainly economic reports for a period of transition after the National Socialist regime had been overthrown. The planned final report was never published because of the arrest of the Freiburgers. This final report was actually meant for Goerdeler – although not all its members were aware of this.

The Freiburg School was essentially concerned with overcoming the problems of the fascist central-planning system. They are chiefly of interest because it was their ideas about a "Free Market Economy" which began to be applied in the Federal Republic of Germany in 1948. Ludwig Erhard (later

to become Chancellor), for example, was a junior member of the group.

One other resistance group that had loose connections with the Freiburg School and the Wednesday Club was the Solf Circle,

which got its name from the widow of the former German Ambassador to Japan, Wilhelm Solf. Opposition officials from within the German Foreign Office occasionally met at her home. The circle was by no

One reason why Hitler and the Nazis appealed to the German middle classes was "because the authoritarian conscience was too deeply embedded in the collective psyche of the German people" (Klaus Fischer).

Carl Friedrich Goerdeler, Mayor of Leipzig (1930–37), was an anti-Nazi who used his position as overseas representative of the Bosch company to enlist the support of Britain, France and the USA against Hitler, but failed.

means a seriously conspiratorial group with the intention to assassinate Hitler. Its members met to exchange free opinions unconstrained by the political, intellectual and cultural principles of National Socialism. Some of these attended a birthday party given by Elizabeth von Thadden who, like Hanna Solf, had helped victims of political and racial persecution escape to Switzerland. The Gestapo had been tipped-off by one of the participants, the Berlin physician Dr Paul Reckzeh, who turned out to be an informant for the Gestapo and who had been compiling reports about the group and its discussions hostile to the regime. Reckzeh had agreed to transport incriminating letters to Switzerland. When Count von Moltke warned the circle in September 1943 that Dr Reckzeh was a Gestapo agent, it was already too late.

During the course of 1944, the Gestapo arrested nearly all members of the group. Elizabeth von Thadden and Otto Kiep, a Foreign Office official, were sentenced to death by the People's Court for "undermining the national defence effort" and attempting high treason. Hanna Solf and her daughter, Countess Lagi von Ballestrem, owed their lives to the intercession of the Japanese Ambassador in Berlin. Other members of the Solf Circle who had connections with Goerdeler and Moltke were either executed in the aftermath of the 20 July attempt on Hitler's life or later by the

> ## As a rule, bourgeois resistance was comprised of originally pro-Nazi personalities

SS. The spirit of the circle was encapsulated by Nikolaus von Halem, who shouted at Roland Freisler who had just sentenced him to death: "A ship can go down, but it doesn't have to haul down its flag."

Perhaps the most famous bourgeois, or national-conservative, resistance group was the so-called "Kreisau Circle". This was a younger group than either the Wednesday Club or the Freiburg Circle, so named by the Gestapo after 20 July because some of its meetings had taken place at Helmuth von Moltke's family estate at Kreisau in the Lower Silesian county of Schweidnitz. The Kreisau Circle had begun to form after 1940 and, in fact, many important meetings took place in Berlin. Moltke was the moving spirit of this group, which consisted of conservatives, socialists, rural estate owners, trade unionists, Protestants and Catholics. Although it did not hold formal meetings, the Kreisau group numbered about 25 people, with a further 30 more individuals who were loosely connected to the group. Members of the Kreisau Circle refrained

from formal membership, although Moltke did attempt to commit the various parties and individuals to common principles in order to establish as wide a consensus as possible. The Kreisau Circle established contacts with other oppositionist circles, such as the resistance group within the *Abwehr* (Counterintelligence Office), the Solf, Sperr and Freiburg Circles, and the Munich Jesuits.

HELMUTH VON MOLTKE

Helmuth James Graf von Moltke was born in 1907 at Kreisau. He studied agriculture and law and inherited the family estate when he was very young. He travelled extensively and acquired enlightened and liberal views of society. His mother was English, and he developed close links with Britain. He was an imposing man of six feet seven inches tall, slim, ascetic, dryly humourous who enjoyed the simple pleasures of life. As a rule, bourgeois resistance was comprised of personalities who had, at least in part, initially supported National Socialist policy. The later conspirators progressed through varying degrees of disenchantment with the regime before taking up active resistance. Moltke was an exception to the rule and was never a Nazi. In fact, he was one of the few members of the upper class who never felt any sympathy for Nazism's objectives. In the presidential elections of 1932 he voted communist; on 30 January 1933 he never went along with the prevailing upper class view that accession to power would reveal Hitler's incompetence and he would consequently be ousted after a short period in office. Like the social democrats, he saw that voting for Hitler was tantamount to voting for war. He never waivered in his view. However, his Christian beliefs prevented him from having anything to do with plans to assassinate Hitler, believing instead that

Goerdeler on trial following the failure of the July 1944 Bomb Plot. He had drawn up a provisional government list for a Germany after Hitler's death, with himself pencilled in as Chancellor. He was hanged at Plötzensee in February 1945.

Nazism would have to run its course. Moltke was well aware that he was not in a position to overthrow National Socialism. Early in the war he is alleged to have said to a member of the von Stauffenberg (see Chapter 7) family: "We are not conspirators, we're not capable of being, we've not learnt how to do it, we shouldn't try to make a start now, it would go wrong, we should make an amateur job of it." Eventually, however, he would look to the military to apply force even if he had little confidence that it would do so. Moltke's perception of human freedom, dignity, rights and justice made him an adversary of National Socialism from the outset. During the war he worked in the Counterintelligence Office in the German High Command, serving as an advisory expert for wartime and international law. He refused persistently to give the

Hitler salute and once prevented the swastika flag from being hoisted on his office building in Berlin. He also gave assistance to Jews, prisoners-of-war and the civilian populations of occupied Europe. In the summer of 1940, Moltke began to assemble a small group of mostly conservatives and landowners who held similar views to himself. These included Otto von Gablentz, Theodor Steltzer and Eugen Gerstenmaier. Eventually the Kreisau Circle was extended to include liberals, socialists and trade unionists. All the individuals drawn to the

> *A cross-section of anti-Nazi German society should prepare for reconstruction*

group agreed that the Hitler regime was bound to collapse, and that a representative cross-section of anti-Nazi German society should prepare for reconstruction and be ready to serve the nation. They modified their position only after witnessing the escalating crimes committed by the regime and the destructive effects of the war, which led them to fear the "Bolshevization" of the German people and the complete destruction of Western civilization.

The Kreisau Circle had no plans of its own for a *coup d'état*, but it did have contacts through individual members to different resistance groups. One was the lawyer Count Peter Yorck von Wartenburg, three years older than Moltke, a deeply religious man who had connections with military circles. Another original member of the group was Adam von Trott zu Solz, a former Oxford (Rhodes) scholar with close links to the German Foreign Office. Trott

was particularly keen to secure British and American support for oppositional groups to Hitler. Trott and Yorck came from the same aristocratic élite as Moltke, but all sorts of people were drawn to the Kreisau Circle. They included Horst von Einsiedel, an economist and social democrat; Moltke's cousin, Carl Dietrich von Trotha, a lawyer, economist and Christian socialist; Prussian conservatives like Count Friedrich Detlev von der Schulenburg, Count Ulrich von Schwerin-Schwanenfeld and Hans Bernd von Haeften; Theodor Steltzer, the former Rendensburg district magistrate; the agricultural scientist Fritz Chritiansen-Weniger; Professor Hans Peters, a jurist affiliated with the Centre Party; Fathers Alfred Delp, Lothar König and Augustin Rösch; the socialists Professor Adolf Reichwein (the group's chief adviser on education), Theo Haubach, Julius Leber, Wilhelm Leuschner, and Carlo Mierendorff; Harold Poelchau, a Protestant minister in the Berlin-Tegel prison; and Jakob Kaiser from the Christian Trade Unions. All these men turned to Moltke as the natural leader of a sort of debating society imbued with strong Christian ethics. Nearly all of them were to be murdered by the Nazis.

LINKS WITH THE CHURCHES

In 1941, Moltke made a concerted effort to win over the churches. Of his numerous contacts with high Catholic officials (including Faulhaber in Munich, Bertram in Breslau and Gröber in Freiburg), the one with bishop Count Preysing of Berlin proved to be the most valuable (see Chapter 5). Eugen Gerstenmaier, who worked in the Foreign Office but had been a member of the Ecclesiastical Foreign Office of the evangelical church, made contact with Theophil Wurm, state bishop in Württemberg, and one of the few advocates

German prisoners on the Eastern Front in the winter of 1941–42. Middle class anti-Nazis hoped that the dreadful losses suffered in Russia would shake support for Hitler, but they were to be sadly disappointed.

of resistance among Protestants. However, discussions with the various bishops quickly revealed that the German churches were not prepared to resist the National Socialist regime openly.

Moltke's own views of the situation under National Socialism appear in a long letter he wrote to a British friend (Lionel Curtis) in 1942. In it he spoke bleakly of the constant danger facing conspiratorial groups and of the release of the "beast in man". However, he also saw optimistic signs of a "religious awakening" that was accompanied "by a readiness if need be for death". Moltke and his Kreisau friends were indeed witness to such a movement. "Today," he

"visualise Europe after the war". To this end the Kreisau Circle held three important meetings, in the spring of 1942, the autumn of 1942 and the spring of 1943. They produced a document entitled *The Fundamental Principles of the New Order*, of which the latest draft dates from August 1943. Its authors were Moltke and Yorck, and it summarizes the conclusions of the three large Kreisau meetings and presents a programme for Germany's rebuilding in the spirit of Christianity. The first large meeting of the circle was on Whit Sunday 1942, and was dedicated to the relations between church and state, specifically to the Concordat (see Chapter 5), and the reform

> *Moltke and his friends believed that Germany had to seek a new spiritual integration*

of the educational and university system. The second meeting in October 1942 addressed the future structure of the state and the economy. The final meeting in June 1943 touched on questions related to the economy, but was concerned primarily with the punishment of National Socialist war criminals by special courts (a certain irony in the light of the Nuremberg War Crimes Tribunals held in 1945–46).

Moltke and his friends believed that Germany had to seek a new spiritual integration on the basis of Christianity, and must overcome the divisions of class, religion and political persuasion. That participation in communal affairs was both a right and a duty. The group believed it was necessary to decentralize and delegate as much decision-making as possible to a local level, and furthermore to incorporate into

wrote, "not a numerous, but an active part of the German people are beginning to realize, not that they have been led astray, not that bad times await them, not that the war may end in defeat, but that what is happening is sin and that they are personally responsible for each terrible deed that has been committed – naturally, not in the earthly sense, but as Christians."

In view of the situation, Moltke and his co-conspirators saw it as their task to the community those, especially workers, who had hitherto been treated in Germany as outsiders. As a consequence of these two principles, they called for the nationalization of key industries, the break-up of large corporations, and the participation of company workforces in management planning and company profits. In other words, the economic and social life was to be built upwards from the smallest units, to be small enough to be manageable (the exact opposite of the National Socialist state). They remained convinced of the value of a "democracy of the grass roots" and of the necessity of building up representative politics from below. The group was also suspicious of political parties and even of trade unions as lobbyists promoting self-interest at the expense of the nation. This

idea did not sit easily with the views of group members such as Julius Leber, who believed that the workers were not merely an indispensable pillar of society but the bedrock on which the whole fate of the nation rested. Moltke's idea of replacing employer-employee confrontation at higher levels by delegates chosen by both sides of industry at lower levels provoked bitter debate with Leber, who found some of the ideas of the Kreisau Group patronizing. Moltke considered that he was helping the workers by giving them equal status; Leber

The walls of Ravensbrück concentration camp, near Berlin, where Count Graf Helmuth von Moltke, a leading member of the Kreisau Circle, was incarcerated following his capture by the Gestapo in January 1944.

The crematorium at Ravensbrück. Just before his execution von Moltke wrote: "Ever since National Socialism came to power, I have done my best to mitigate the consequences for its victims and prepared for a change."

the first system of government to be established after Hitler's overthrow would not be sufficiently radical enough to maintain the aspirations of the people, thus opening the door to Russian-style communism. It was agreed, however, that the first parliament was to be formed without the participation of political parties

> ## This procedure was known as a "constructive vote of no confidence"

and would consist of elected individuals from regional and municipal representative assemblies. The *Reichstag* would not choose the Chancellor, instead it would ratify the choice of a Head of State (Reich Regent). To prevent an unscrupulous Chancellor from remaining in power indefinitely with the backing of the Regent, the *Reichstag* could call for the Chancellor's dismissal – but had to agree on a new Chancellor immediately. This procedure was known as a "constructive vote of no confidence" and was written into the Constitution of the Federal Republic of Germany in 1949. The Kreisau proposals were aimed as much at avoiding the polarization of politics under the Weimar Republic as they were to prevent a repeat of unbridled political power and terror under the Third Reich.

In the months leading up to the publication of *The Fundamental Principles of the New Order*, leading figures within the Kreisau Circle were formulating not only their vision of a post-Hitler Germany but how this could in practice be facilitated. Allied support – or more specifically, Western Allied support – was crucial, they believed, in preventing the workers (and

wanted a society in which they took the decisions. Moltke came to regard Julius Leber as a "convincingly good man who at any rate keeps a firm grip on the purely practical and attaches a good deal less importance to things of the mind than I do". Both Moltke and Leber were concerned that

Some of those anti-Hitler individuals discussed in this chapter came before Roland Freisler, President of the People's Court. A rabid Nazi, he believed that judges in reaching their decisions should put themselves in the shoes of the Führer.

activities. Trott in particular was able to take advantage of his official position in the Counterintelligence Office to make a number of trips abroad. In April 1942, he went to Geneva where he entrusted to Dr Hooft (Secretary of the Provisional Committee of the World Council of Churches and a friend of his mother) with a letter intended for Sir Stafford Cripps (at that time Lord Privy Seal in the British Cabinet). The letter outlined the composition and thinking of the Kreisau Circle and its conspiratorial activities in the face of intense Gestapo terror, and warned of the threat posed by the Soviet Union, particularly in the light of the uncertainty of British and American attitudes towards a change of government in Germany. The document ended with a plea for dialogue, coupled with a common recognition of the international failure to deal in a Christian manner with complex political, cultural and economic factors that had brought the world to its present situation. Cripps passed the letter to Winston Churchill, who wrote on it "Most encouraging". A verbal reply was sent back to Trott welcoming further dialogue, but firmly ruling out all prospects of negotiating the shape of a post-war settlement until Germany had been defeated militarily.

DISAPPOINTMENT

Moltke, like others within "Kreisau" (especially Trott), accepted the premise that Germany would and must be defeated. However, Moltke was as unsuccessful as other resistance emissaries in securing Western support. In 1943, Moltke tried to speak with representatives of the Allies through Turkey during his visits to Istanbul in July and December 1943, concerning the possibility of capitulation on the Western Front. Moltke argued that given the existing situation and the unacceptable behaviour of the Red Army in Poland and the Baltic

others) from falling under communist influence. Moltke, together with Haeften and von Trott, who had been given special responsibility for foreign affairs, made determined efforts to make contact with the British and Americans in order to secure their support for their conspiratorial

States, the Western Allied presence would have to offset the real possibility of German occupation by the Red Army. He proposed an internal coup on condition that the Western Allies occupied Germany swiftly after the coup. During a further visit to Geneva in April 1944, Trott suggested to Allen Dulles (Chief OSS representative in Switzerland) that the Anglo-Americans should make a number of statements in order to reassure German workers that labour would be given a privileged place in post-war Germany, and that Germany would be allowed to settle its own affairs without outside interference. He also wanted

> ## Western politicians remained distrustful of the German "aristocratic clique"

the Allies to give a promise that they did not intend to establish a puppet government in Germany that would implement Allied interests at the expense of the German people. Trott remained convinced that unless these assurances were forthcoming, then there was every likelihood that large sections of Germany would succumb to communist influence. At the time, Anglo-Americans did not believe that these fears were serious enough to warrant a major departure from their established policies. Western politicians remained profoundly distrustful of the oppositional German "aristocratic clique", even to the point of contempt. They continued to insist on unconditional surrender.

In the course of the Gestapo's investigations of the Counterintelligence Office, von Moltke was arrested on 19 January 1944 and sent to Ravensbrück concentration camp for having warned retired Consul General Kiep, employed at the time in the Foreign Relations section of the German Army High Command and a member of the Solf Circle, that he had been placed on the Gestapo's wanted list. After Leber and Reichwein were turned in by an informer for having contacts with a communist group, von Yorck and Haubach pushed the military to carry out the assassination of Hitler quickly (see Chapter 7). Yorck, Trott zu Solz and Haeften offered their assistance to the assassins on 20 July 1944. Moltke's offence was a minor one and the authorities remained unaware of most of the activities in which he had been engaged. The activities of Moltke did not even come to light in the proceedings held against him before the notorious People's Court of Roland Freisler. After the failed attempt on Hitler's life, von Moltke's wife visited him in prison, when he is alleged to have said: "If I had been free, this would not have happened." His last letter to his sons said that he had "never wished for or contributed to acts of violence like that of 20 July ... because I ... believed that the fundamental spiritual evil would not be got rid of in that way." It is conceivable, had he been at liberty during the dramatic months leading up to July, that Moltke may have changed his mind – like several of his friends within the Kreisau Circle, who had become convinced that the assassination of Hitler offered the only chance of securing a quick end to the war. During the ensuing grotesque trials of the conspirators, von Moltke's own involvement began to emerge.

However, despite collecting a considerable dossier of his conspiratorial activities, the authorities found themselves in a difficult position. On the one hand Moltke had been incarcerated since January and could not have taken an active role in the plot to kill Hitler, and furthermore Moltke could point to his Christian faith and his well-known opposition to murder. He was therefore charged only with taking part in consultations on Germany's political reconstruction after the defeat of National Socialism together with like-minded individuals – in effect, for having thought and talked about a non-Nazi Germany.

MOLTKE'S MOTIVATION

In two remarkable letters describing his trial, which he wrote to his wife between his sentence on 10 January 1945 and execution on the 23rd, Moltke said that he was to die precisely for those things for which he was really responsible, not for actions of any kind or conspiracies, but for his thoughts ("we are to be hanged for thinking together"). In his second letter he praised the merciful dispensation of God which had "removed" him from active participation in the Putsch preparations, and had separated him from all class interests and all patriotic motives so that he could testify to the deepest force of the resistance. He stood before Freisler, he wrote: "not as a Protestant, not as a great landowner, not as an aristocrat, not as a Prussian, not as a German ... but as a Christian and as nothing else." This has been widely interpreted as an admission that he did nothing but think, whereas his work for the victims of Nazism and his links with conspirators in the military and elsewhere suggest that he took action whenever possible. In his farewell letter to his sons, Moltke wrote with characteristic eloquence and forcefulness: "Throughout my life from my schooldays onwards I have fought against a spirit of narrowness and subservience, of arrogance and intolerance, against the absolutely merciless consistency which is deeply ingrained in the Germans and has found its expression in the National Socialist state. I have made it my aim to get this spirit overcome with its evil accompaniments, such as excessive nationalism, racial persecution, lack of faith and materialism. In this sense and seen from their own standpoint the National Socialists are right in putting me to death ... Ever since National Socialism came to power, I have done my best to mitigate the consequences for its victims and prepared for a change: I was driven to do so by my conscience and in the last resort that is a task worth a man's life."

Writing after the war, the American diplomat George Kennan paid tribute to Moltke as a "pillar of moral conscience and an unfailing source of political and intellectual inspiration". Helmuth von Moltke was a true German in the sense that he, from the standpoint of an absolute belief in Christian principles, became an implacable and unconditional enemy of National Socialism. He died for his beliefs on 23 January 1945 at Plötzensee prison. Seven members of the Kreisau Circle were hanged for their participation in the 20 July 1944 conspiracy: Yorck, Reichwein, Trott, Haeften, Haubach, Leber and Father Delp, who was the last person of the Kreisau Circle to be executed in February 1945.

THE KREISAU CONTRIBUTION

There was probably never more than 20 to 25 active members of the Kreisau Circle, but it had almost as many sympathizers with important connections to all aspects of German society. Terence Prittie has likened the effect of the Kreisau Circle to a stone dropped into a stagnant pool, with ripples running outwards and onwards. Whereas the generals had to organize action to rid Germany of Hitler, Kreisau produced the moral and intellectual ideas which gave them faith and a sense of moral legitimacy. Moreover, the influence of the "Kreisauers" continued after the war, and the intellectual vigour of their discussions and thought made a substantial contribution to the rebuilding of post-war Germany.

Freisler in action. Under him the number of death sentences delivered by the People's Court increased from 102 in 1941 to 2097 in 1944. He was killed in a US bombing raid on Berlin whilst delivering a sentence in February 1945.

As time went on, the views of the various middle class, national-conservative resistance groups drew closer together. But a fundamental difference remained between the views of the Wednesday Club and the Kreisau Circle. Goerdeler, Beck and von Hassel were determined to restore as much as possible of the pre-Hitler Germany (and even the pre-1914 Germany) and to avoid unconditional surrender – at least to all three of the Allies at the same time. In other words, the aims of the Wednesday Club, the Freiburg School and the "Kreisauers" reflect different generational attitudes and outlooks. The older bourgeois conservatives found it difficult to accept that the political and economic costs of defeat in World War I meant that the map of Europe could not be redrawn to ensure the survival of the old aristocratic status quo. The "Kreisauers", on the other hand, consisted of a younger Christian and intellectual élite that was prepared for Germany to be defeated "unconditionally" because they believed that only with a clean slate could Germany begin to reconstruct along liberal-democratic lines. Moltke and other members of the Kreisau group regarded unequivocal military defeat as a moral and political necessity for the future of the nation – even at the risk of their being subjected to accusations of treason from their fellow countrymen.

RESISTANCE AND THE CHURCHES

The story of the churches in Germany during the 1930s and their resistance to the Nazi regime is one of weakness and lack of resolve, redeemed only by the actions of a few brave individuals.

The Nazi attitude towards the churches in Germany was both confused and inconsistent, and characterized by fundamental hostility in outlook and considerable local persecution. At first the Nazi Party

Pope Pius XI, who signed the Concordat with the Nazi government in July 1933 which assured German citizens freedom to profess and practise religion, and guaranteed the legal status of the church in return for its non-interference in politics.

percent of Germans (almost 22 million people) were Catholic.

When the NSDAP gained power in 1933, it was not seen by either the Protestant or the Catholic Church as a particular call for protest or resistance. On the contrary, both churches viewed the overthrow of the pluralist, "decadent" Weimar Republic with delight and looked forward in anticipation to a restoration of traditional German values. Protest by church leaders that did take place was invariably directed against certain interests of the National Socialist authorities, but not against the state; indeed, most forms of muted protest were accompanied with the affirmation that the protest served the state. By and large, the church leadership observed the Nazis' actions in the social and political spheres with sympathy, as exemplified by the 12 November 1933 pastoral letter by the Bavarian bishops, which speaks of saving the German people from the "horrors of Bolshevism". "Resistance" or "dissent" by church leaders was confined to matters of the church. There was strict division between the sphere of the church, in which the state was not to become involved, and the sphere of the state, in which the church was not to become involved.

Hitler and senior Nazi leaders believed religion and National Socialism to be irreconcilable. However, Catholicism and the Confessional Church were strong influences in many Germans' lives, so the Nazis had to proceed carefully.

JEHOVAH'S WITNESSES

The only religious group that fought National Socialist coercions with comparable determination and obstinacy were the Jehovah's Witnesses, who were outlawed just a few months after the National Socialist "seizure of power". The Nazis viewed the Jehovah's Witnesses as a serious threat to its notion of "people and state", as the latter were unwilling to give unquestioning loyalty to the Nazi state. The resolute disobedience of Jehovah's Witnesses to comply with Nazi obligations to give the

attempted to identify National Socialism with Christianity but later declared the two beliefs to be irreconcilable. Even though Hitler may have been fundamentally hostile to the Christian churches by 1933, he had no definite idea of how to proceed against them. In 1933, for example, 62.7 percent of the population (i.e. over 40 million people) belonged to one of the country's 28 independent Protestant churches, and 32.4

Hitler salute, to take oaths of allegiance, and to become members of National Socialist youth and labour organizations etc, led to a clear escalation of conflict and religious persecution. The first mass arrests of Jehovah's Witnesses occurred in 1935–36 in the Rhine and Ruhr areas. From 1936, Jehovah's Witnesses were increasingly deprived in custody hearings of their right to raise their children. Housing provisions for children then opened the way for the imprisonment of their mothers as well. If Jehovah's Witnesses did not agree to leave their religious community by the end of their sentence at the latest, then they were threatened with hard labour or concentration camp. Husbands were generally imprisoned, which left many women to take on and coordinate missionary activities. This meant that they could expect no further mercy from the Gestapo or from the courts if they were arrested again. Of the 25,000 Jehovah's Witnesses in the Third Reich, about 10,000 were imprisoned for various periods of time, 2000 of them in concentration camps. Approximately 250 were executed, primarily by *Wehrmacht* court convictions for refusing to serve in the armed forces. However, their activity was not directed towards changing the political order; rather, they were concerned to secure unrestricted religious freedom. It is therefore difficult to place the opposition of Jehovah's Witnesses within a ruling paradigm, as for them "resistance" was a binding act of religious faith.

Pastor Ludwig Müller, the nationalistic and anti-Semitic priest who became a leading figure in the association of German Christians and a friend of leading Nazi army officers. He was elected Reich Bishop of the Protestant Church in 1933.

THE PROTESTANT CHURCH

In the case of Protestantism, which bore a Lutheran mark, the reasons for its lack of resistance were largely derived from history. The Evangelical Church comprised nearly 60 percent of the German people, but in terms of resistance it was inhibited by its past. It stood in a 400-year-old tradition of mutual respect between state and church ("throne and altar"), a cosy relationship that had created a traditional Christian respect for authority, both among the clergy and their congregations. This is a reference to the fact that the Evangelical Church was divided up into 28 mutually independent state churches and the Prussian Lutheran tradition, which produced a strong propensity for nationalistic aberrations. The Protestant Church, weakened by serious internal divisions, was

> ## *The Evangelical Church comprised nearly 60 percent of the German people*

obliged in July 1933 to accept a new constitution which rapidly became the means of forcing the church under state control. It was further weakened by a radical breakaway movement known as the "German Christians", who adopted Nazi form and style and called for the creation of a new "People's Church" that could identify with the *Volk*. Accusing the two main branches of the Protestant Church – the Lutheran and Reformed – of having lost touch with the people, the German Christians, campaigning for control under the slogan "the swastika on our breasts and the cross in our hearts", gradually began to undermine the fabric of the established Protestant Church.

SS soldiers on parade. Great pressure was brought to bear by the Nazi hierarchy on members of the SS to renounce all ties to organized religion, as Hitler saw National Socialism as a religious faith itself.

When, in May 1933, in accordance with the Nazi principle of *Gleichschaltung* (obligatory assimilation into the state of all political, economic and cultural activities), Pastor Friedrich von Bodelschingh was elected National Bishop by the church officials, the German Christians, under the control of Pastor Joachim Hossenfelder, protested along with their candidate, Pastor Ludwig Müller, and insisted that the election

Pastor Martin Niemöller of the Confessional Church. At first this World War I submarine commander and holder of the *Pour le Mérite* thought that Hitler would be good for Germany, but became quickly disillusioned.

be carried out by the overall church membership. When the church bodies were newly elected on 23 July 1933 the German Christians, calling themselves the "Storm Troopers of Jesus Christ" and with the support of Hitler, won easily. This gave them control of the State Synod, which duly elected Ludwig Müller, an ex-army chaplain, National Bishop on 1 October 1933.

PROTESTANT ANTI-NAZIS

In spite of the widespread Protestant enthusiasm for the Nazis, there existed a few small, isolated groups that remained sceptical and were not prepared to support National Socialist policy. These groups included members of the Religious Socialists (such as Emil Fuchs), the Liberal Protestants (such as Martin Rade and Hermann Mulert), some defenders of dialectical theology, and several very different representatives from the Lutheran section (such as Hermann Sasse and Dietrich Bonhöffer). These groups tended to be motivated by political ideology, having been for the most part active in the SPD and the German Democratic Party (DDP) in Weimar. The Lutherans, on the other hand, were primarily theologically motivated and were opposed to the rise of dictatorship. The employees of the Foreign Contact Office of the German Evangelical Church should also be mentioned. Among them was Eugen Gerstenmaier, a member of the Kreisau Circle and a church leader. These people were in constant danger because they used their connections to pass on information and to help victims of persecution to flee the country. Although these groups were powerless and isolated, they nonetheless fall into a rare category of church groups that were able to see National Socialism for what it was.

Clerical protest arose out of the desire for theological and ethical autonomy, in defence against control by the Nazi state, and in the attempt to escape the centralizing process of *Gleichschaltung*. This protest took the form not only of non-conformity and passive resistance but also more organized, active oppositional acts.

Opposition in pursuit of clerical autonomy can be seen in the response of certain sections within the Protestant Church as early as 1933. The Nazis' attempt to "coordinate" it and the election of the pro-Nazi Pastor Müller elicited a spirited response coordinated by Pastor Martin Niemöller, the best-known German clergyman of the twentieth century. In 1933, Niemöller had welcomed the Nazi regime

> **The Confessional Church did not protest at the exclusion of Jews from national life**

and supported Hitler's goal of restoring Germany's national prestige abroad. At the same time he opposed plans by the German Christians to seize control of the ecclesiastical hierarchy and to impose pro-Nazi policies in theology and practice. In September 1933, Niemöller wrote a letter to his fellow clergymen that was to provide the initial impetus for the Confessional Church and its struggle in subsequent years to preserve the church's institutional autonomy. In opposition to the German Christians' intention to introduce an "Aryan paragraph" in church practice, that is, exclude Christian Jews from the church, Niemöller joined forces with those who shared his convictions to form the Pastors' Emergency League. The Confessional Church, which arose in opposition to the

In January 1934, Hermann Göring accused Niemöller of attempting to drive a wedge between President Hindenburg and Hitler. However, the tough priest refused to be bullied by Hitler and his henchmen.

pro-Nazi German Christian Church, did not protest at the exclusion of Jews from national life, but rather objected to the denominational breach that it perceived in the ecclesiastical Aryan paragraph. The Pastors' Emergency League was inaugurated

Niemöller's Confessional Church came out against the Nazis' actions and their anti-Semitism. For his outspoken resistance Niemöller was arrested in 1937 and served his sentence in various concentration camps, but survived the war.

with the object of helping anyone persecuted in contravention of the Christian faith, as set out in the scriptures and in the Reformation Confessions which interpreted them.

In mid-November 1933 the League numbered 3000 members. By mid-January 1934, membership had risen to just over 7000, nearly half of all the Evangelical pastors in Germany. Yet within a month of its formation, Niemöller and four other Berlin pastors who had played an important part in setting it up sent Hitler a telegram congratulating him on his "manly act to preserve Germany's honour by leaving the League of Nations" in October 1933. They wanted to make it clear that they accepted his leadership in other walks of life provided he did not insist on assuming complete control of the churches.

In the meantime, the German Christians held a mass rally in the Sportspalast in Berlin, at which a crowd of 20,000 heard demands for the creation of a "People's Church"

> *A representative group of church leaders called on Hitler with a list of complaints*

(*Volkskirche*) which would eliminate all Jewish elements in its faith. Niemöller played a leading role in compelling the Reich Bishop, Müller, to condemn the German Christians' views which had been expanded at the Sportspalast, and to force Hossenfelder to resign as President of the German Christians. For his part, Müller retaliated with a "Muzzling Degree" which forbade the introduction of church politics into religious services and criticism of the church leadership. He also, without any consultation, surrendered the church youth groups to the Hitler Youth. As a result, in January 1934, a representative group of church leaders called on Hitler with a list of complaints. At the meeting which took place on 25 January Niemöller, who had been accused by Göring of driving a wedge between President Hindenburg and Hitler, defended himself by claiming that his only concern was the welfare of the church, state and German people. Hitler replied: "You confine yourself to the church, I'll take care of the German people." As Niemöller was leaving the meeting he spoke up to Hitler and said: "We, too, as Christians and churchmen, have a responsibility to the German people which was entrusted to us by God. Neither you nor anyone else in the world has the power to take it from us." Although such plain speaking was typical of the pugnacious Niemöller, he was reproached afterwards by his fellow clergy for having strengthened Ludwig Müller's hand. Hitler certainly was unaccustomed to being spoken to so forcibly, and he incurred the Führer's lasting animosity. On 26 January Niemöller was suspended from office, and on 10 February superannuated from his Berlin-Dahlem parish. Two thousand pastors immediately left the League. However, his parishioners decided to back him and he was able to continue to campaign vigorously against the Nazis' ecclesiastical schemes.

THE CONFESSIONAL CHURCH

Following the meeting with Hitler in January, the bishops of the state churches submitted themselves to the authority of the National Bishop (Müller) in the hope that conciliation would save the unity of the German Evangelical Church. However, the church membership was not prepared to go along with this. When Müller overplayed his hand and turned against Bishop Theopil Wurm of Württemberg, who had bent over backwards to be conciliatory, this provoked a meeting in April of Protestants from all over Germany at Ulm which led on to the foundation of the Confessional Church. Free synods were formed which, in contrast to the official church, funded and trained their

pastors themselves. On 31 May 1934, the Synod of the Confessional Church met in Barmen and adopted the Barmen Theological Declaration that affirmed that Jesus, as attested in scripture, is the ultimate source of authority. In rejecting the German Christians' heretical theology, the Confessional Church also distanced itself from the National Socialist state. Niemöller had not played a leading part in producing the Barmen Declaration, but he defended its principles whenever accused by pro-Nazi theologians of spreading false doctrines. When a further Synod in October 1934, held in Niemöller's parish of Dahlem, declared the Confessional Church to be the only legal one in Germany and commissioned the Council of Brethren to act on its behalf, he was one of the six members of the Executive Committee which the Council established.

Hitler was forced to realize that his plan to create a National Socialist Evangelical Church under Bishop Müller was untenable. Now the Gestapo was given free rein in dealing with the Confessional Church and other dissident church leaders. Distribution of the Barmen Declaration was prohibited and the text was seized. Without actually wanting to do so, the Confessional Church came into direct confrontation with the National Socialist state. It was forced to undertake the main burden of the Evangelical Church "struggle" and was pushed underground. Its messages were printed and distributed clandestinely, in such places as the basement of the Essen lawyer and Synod member Gustav Heinemann (later President of the Federal Republic of Germany). Gestapo infomers took notes on the sermons preached and pastors were placed in "protective custody", forced to leave the country or incarcerated in concentration camps. In 1935 alone, 500 ministers were placed under temporary arrest. Martin

Niemöller remained the Confessional Church's symbol of opposition and continued to criticize the ecclesiastical policy of the regime in his sermons and lectures. He was arrested in 1937 and arraigned in a highly

The Evangelical Protestant theologian Dietrich Bonhöffer. This photograph was taken during his theology studies in New York (1930–31). He became a pastor, returned to Germany in 1931 but was banned from preaching by Gestapo order.

publicized show trial. Though remarkably acquitted by the court, he was immediately re-arrested and confined as Hitler's "personal prisoner" in the concentration camps of Sachsenhausen and Dachau, from which he was liberated by Allied forces in 1945, only days before he was scheduled to be executed.

WURM'S PROTESTS

While in prison Niemöller's influence naturally declined, however his presence there remained a constant reminder to the rest of the world of the Nazi treatment of dissident clergy. His arrest unquestionably weakened the "resistance" of the Confessional Church and membership of the Pastors' Emergency League continued to fall. The leadership passed to the infinitely more moderate Pastor Wurm, who gradually realized that compromise with such a barbaric regime was not to be had. In 1940, Evangelical state bishops such as Wurm and Hans Meiser (Bavaria) accused the regime of murdering the mentally ill (see page 116), fully aware of the consequences that this could have for them. Wurm in particular continued to protest in numerous petitions to state authorities against the injustices committed by the National Socialists.

Seen as a whole, though, the Confessional Church's protests remained minimal in view of the magnitude of the regime's crimes. When, for example, the Nuremberg Laws in September 1935 heightened discrimination against German Jews, the churches were conspicuous by their silence: they failed to offer a word of protest. Partly, this silence can be explained by the fact that the churches were continuing to fight for their own existence during this period. However, more alarmingly, their failure to respond to such blatant institutionalized discrimination highlights the weakness of their opposition, which was constantly undermined by theological traditions and politico-ideological constraints.

Because the Confessional Church viewed its struggle primarily in ecclesiastical and theological terms, not political ones, it was unable to cooperate with the political resistance movement. Nevertheless, some of its members were aware of the plot against Hitler and indeed were indirectly implicated. Among them were Dietrich Bonhöffer and F.J. Perels, who were both executed shortly before the end of the war.

Bonhöffer died in trying to save his country. He left to posterity an important message of implacable moral and religious resistance to evil. Dietrich Bonhöffer was born in 1906 into a large and influential family of intellectuals and studied theology,

> *Back in Germany in 1931,*
> *Bonhöffer started to teach at*
> *Berlin University*

largely under the influence of Karl Barth, and took up an academic career at the University of Berlin. His international experience and sympathies were heightened by a year's study at the Union Theological Seminary in New York in 1930–31, where one of his teachers was Reinhold Niebuhr. Back in Germany in 1931, he began to teach at Berlin University, worked as a students' chaplain and, at a meeting in Cambridge in Great Britain, was appointed by the World Alliance for Promoting International Friendship through the Churches (the forerunner of the World Council of Churches) as one of its three European Youth Secretaries.

Bonhöffer was arrested in April 1943 (he is shown here in prison in Berlin in 1944) by the *Sicherheitsdienst* (SD), the state's intelligence and security body. He was executed in Flossenbürg in April 1945.

Pope Pius XI, disillusioned with the reality of Nazi rule in Germany, issued the *Mit brennender Sorge* in 1937, an outspoken attack on Nazi beliefs and methods, which contrasts sharply with the silence of his successor, Pope Pius XII.

By the time the Nazis came to power in 1933, his character was such that a collision with the regime seemed inevitable. From the outset he deeply opposed its dictatorial and racial beliefs and became one of the leading young supporters of the Confessional Church which, as we have seen, sought to prevent the introduction of Nazi practices

> *An unconditional obligation towards victims of state-sponsored terrorism*

into the Evangelical Church. Bonhöffer's twin sister Sabine had married a Jewish lawyer named Leibholz, and it was the Aryan clause excluding the Jews from the civil service that persuaded Dietrich to point out the incompatibility of National Socialism with Christianity. He rapidly came to the view that the church had an unconditional obligation towards victims of state-sponsored oppression, and therefore in certain circumstances it was the duty of the church to interfere with the state (what he called "putting a spoke in the wheel") in order to protect such victims. This represented a radical departure from the established Lutheran position. From 1933 to 1935, Bonhöffer served as a Lutheran chaplain in London, where he provided information on Nazism to leaders of the Ecumenical Movement, such as Bishop George Bell of Chichester, in their efforts to mitigate the church struggle in Germany. In 1935 Bonhöffer was brought back from London and put in charge of an unofficial, later illegal, training seminary at Finkenwalde near Stettin for Confessional Church students.

As the position of the church deteriorated, Dietrich Bonhöffer became increasingly despondent and initially sought a position outside Germany. During his visit to Britain in April he had explained to Niebuhr his problems. Niebuhr immediately secured him a post in America. Bonhöffer arrived in the United States in June 1939, but realized that emigration was not the answer. He wrote to Niebuhr expressing the dilemma facing all Christians in a National Socialist Germany: "I must live through this difficult period of our national history with the Christian people of Germany. I will have no right to participate in the reconstruction of Christian life in Germany after the war if I do not share the trials of this time with my people ... Christians in Germany will have to face the terrible alternative of either willing the defeat of their nation and thereby destroying civilization, or doing nothing. I know which of these alternatives I must choose, but I cannot make that choice from security."

BONHÖFFER AND THE *ABWEHR*

After the outbreak of war in 1939, having returned to Germany, he was recruited though his family connections to be a contact between the military resistance group and foreign churchmen. Bonhöffer's lawyer brother-in-law, Hans Dohnanyi (son of the composer) was deputy to Lieutenant-Colonel (later Brigadier-General) Hans Oster in the *Abwehr* (Counterintelligence Office). At the end of October 1940 Bonhöffer became a member of the *Abwehr* attached to its Munich office. Oster, who was a resolute opponent of Hitler, and his conspirators in the *Abwehr*, including Helmuth Groscurth, Helmuth von Moltke, Josef Müller, von Dohnanyi and Bonhöffer, compiled extensive files about the crimes of National Socialism in the event of an overthrow of the government (see Chapter 7). One of the underlying purposes of Bonhöffer's membership of the *Abwehr* was that he should use his contacts to bring

about an understanding between the German resistance and the Allies. He came to support the assassination of Hitler on the grounds that new methods of oppression justify new types of disobedience. This partly explains his failure to establish closer links with Helmuth von Moltke during their joint

Reinhard Heydrich, Chief of the Reich Security Head Office. Like Hitler, he had a detestation of the churches, and they often talked about how they would deal with the "black crows" (priests) when the war was over.

visit to Norway in April 1942. In May and June 1942, Bonhöffer's position in the *Abwehr* facilitated a meeting with Bishop George Bell in Sigtuna, Sweden. Seeking support for the German resistance, Bonhöffer tried unsuccessfully to elicit a public statement from the British and American governments that they would be prepared to negotiate a compromise peace with a post-Hitler regime. However, the standard Allied response was that Hitler's crimes were so great that the whole of Germany, including the resistance, would have to accept an unconditional "penitential" peace settlement.

The *Abwehr* ceased to be a central link for the resistance when, in April 1943, von Dohnanyi, Müller and Bonhöffer were arrested in conjunction with an investigation

> ## Bonhöffer was sent to the Tegel prison where he remained for 18 months

of a matter involving currency dealing that was intended to help Jews who had been smuggled into Switzerland. On the basis of these suspicions, the Gestapo proceeded to search von Dohnanyi's room on 5 April in the presence of Wilhelm Canaris (see Chapter 7) and Hans Oster, and caught the latter trying to hide three incriminating documents from Bonhöffer. Why Bonhöffer's brother-in-law should have retained these documents remains a mystery. Dohnanyi was taken to SD headquarters; Bonhöffer, Müller, Frau Dohnanyi and Frau Müller were arrested later in the day and Oster was placed under house arrest. Bonhöffer was sent to the Tegel prison where he remained for 18 months. From his prison

cell he was able to smuggle out letters, later published as *Widerstand und Ergebung: Briefe und Aufzeichnungen aus der Haft*, 1953 (published in 1972 as *Letters and Papers from Prison*). Bonhöffer was never brought to trial before the People's Court, instead he was held at the RSHA (Reich Central Security Office) headquarters and then transferred to Buchenwald. On 2 April 1945 he was sent to the Flossenbürg camp. Although it proved difficult to pin treasonable charges on him, the Nazis viewed Bonhöffer as one of their most subversive opponents who was all the more dangerous because his resistance was based on deeply held principles. The decision to put him to death was taken by either Hitler or Kaltenbrunner. He died at Flossenbürg concentration camp on the morning of 9 April along with Canaris and Oster, only days before its liberation by the Americans. Just before his execution he managed to send a farewell message to George Bell: "Tell him that for me this is not the end but the beginning." The camp doctor as Flossenbürg said that he had never witnessed anyone facing death so submissive to the will of God. Von Dohnanyi was executed in Sachsenhausen on the same day. Following the war, Bonhöffer's status as an implacable anti-Nazi martyr gave his ideas an added dimension as a percipient response to the dilemma of how Christians should face the challenge of an evil political regime.

THE CATHOLIC CHURCH

Within ecclesiastical opposition, there are some parallels between the Protestant and Catholic churches, in their motives and methods. For the most part, both churches responded by seeking an accommodation with the regime. The attitude of opponents within the church to National Socialism remained inconsistent, with few examples of

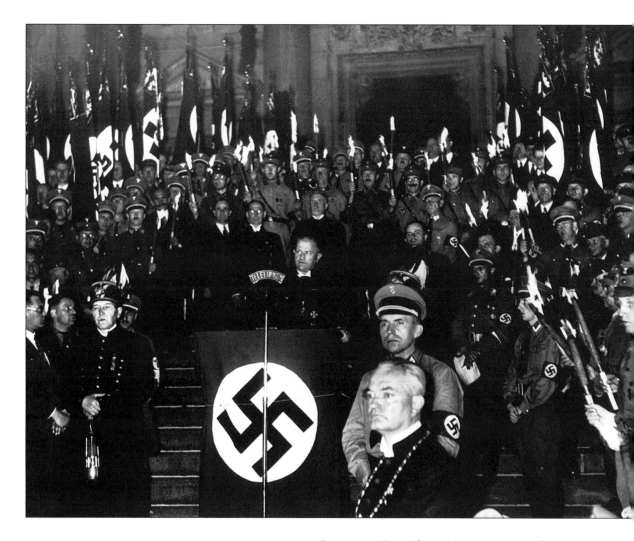

Given the Nazis' dislike of the churches, Bishop Müller, seen here preaching a sermon, quickly became an inconsequential figure in the Third Reich despite being pro-Nazi. He committed suicide in 1946.

coordinated opposition or resistance. The Catholic Church was in some ways in a stronger position to oppose Nazism because it was less divided and also more cosmopolitan. Since Bismarck's *Kulturkampf* (Culture War) of the 1870s, German Catholics had sought to maintain their position within Germany. In July 1933, a Concordat was signed between the National Socialist regime and Rome which allowed the Catholic Church (or so it believed) to retain its autonomous organization. The history of the relations between the regime and the Catholic Church in the years leading up to 1939 is the history of the attempt by the church to assert the privileges granted to it by the Concordat and the attempt by the regime to erode them. Perhaps the clearest example of successful episcopal protest is the church's response (more specifically, a few individuals within

Ernst Kaltenbrunner, Head of the Reich Security Department, was probably responsible for putting Bonhöffer to death at the end of the war. He followed soon after, as he was hanged as a war criminal in October 1946.

the church) to the attempt by the Nazi regime to implement its euthanasia programme. The episcopal protest that this eventually aroused represents a rare example of coordinated action and protest by the two faiths. However before looking at the churches' reaction to the euthanasia campaign, I would like to say something about an important symbolic figure of dissent within the Catholic Church, Bishop Konrad Graf von Preysing.

With the coming of National Socialism, much of the institutional edifice of Catholicism began to crumble. The Catholic Church's famed adaptability, which had helped it to withstand Bismarck's attacks and later to switch with alacrity from monarchical to republican constitutionalism, now served it ill. It is a matter of record that within its own political party (Centre

Party) fewer Catholics than Protestants supported the NSDAP before it came to power; but after January 1933, Catholics, fearing another *Kulturkampf*, attempted to make their peace with the new government. In return for Nazi promises to respect the church's teachings and institutions, the Centre Party voted for the Enabling Act which gave Hitler dictatorial powers and outlawed all other political parties save the NSDAP. Shortly afterwards, during the negotiations for a Concordat between Berlin and the Vatican, the Centre Party voluntarily disbanded itself.

In 1933, Konrad von Preysing, who a year before had been appointed Bishop of Eichstadt in Bavaria, was one of the two

> *Freedom did not mean that bishops or priests could speak out against oppressive policy*

German Bishops to oppose the conclusion of the Concordat (the other being Karl Joseph Schulte of Cologne). With Cardinal Faulhaber of Munich, who was also uneasy, he travelled to Rome to warn the Vatican that a Concordat would not be possible with such a regime. Preysing's warnings had little effect and the Concordat was duly signed on 20 July 1933. It soon became clear that when the Nazis talked of allowing freedom to the Catholic Church, this only included conducting services and administering the sacraments. It did not mean that bishops or priests could speak out against oppressive government policy. The imprecise nature of the agreement soon began to manifest itself when the regime closed down Catholic organizations whose activities were not

Konrad von Preysing, who in 1932 was appointed Bishop of Eichstadt in Bavaria, was one of the two German Bishops to oppose the conclusion of the Concordat (the other being Karl Joseph Schulte of Cologne).

strictly religious. The Catholic press had also to confine itself to purely religious matters, otherwise it too would be censored or banned. Catholic processions could be banned and schools attached to convents

Waffen-SS troops in Russia. Despite the Nazi anti-church campaign, many members of the SS retained their church membership. Even the *Totenkopf* Division, recruited from concentration camp guards, contained believers.

Germany. In August 1935, the bishops' conference at Fulda produced a pastoral letter which agreed that the churches should not interfere in the affairs of the state, although it drew attention to the violations of the Concordat. In 1937 Preysing and Bishop Galen of Münster, together with the Cardinal Archbishops of Breslau, Munich and Cologne, had been called to Rome to review the situation in Germany. The result was the Papal Encyclical *With Burning Anxiety* (*Mit brennender Sorge*) that was smuggled into Germany in March and read from all the Catholic pulpits. Drafted initially by Faulhaber in the name of Pope

It listed the violations of the Concordat and took issue with National Socialism

Pius XI, it listed the violations of the Concordat and took issue with the way National Socialism was both persecuting the Catholic Church and placing political ideology ahead of Christian doctrine. Using the Papal Encyclical, Bishop Preysing called for a more effective idea of defence for the episcopate ("The Public Sphere and Mass Reaction"), especially as the encyclical's wide circulation in Germany had had a liberating effect among Catholic churchgoers. Preysing, who had visited Niemöller a few days before the encyclical, was quite prepared to find himself arrested. He informed a friend: "I said in 1933 that the time would certainly come when we would have to break away, the only question would be when to choose." However, Cardinal Adolf Bertram, chairman of the Catholic bishops' conference, pulled back from any church protest actions that could

were closed, while nuns teaching in German state schools were dismissed. By the end of 1936, Catholic youth groups had been managing to assemble only on strictly church occasions.

While Preysing (who had been appointed Bishop of Berlin in 1935) and a few other clergy continued to oppose the Nazis, the Vatican failed in the main to intervene on behalf of the 22 million Roman Catholics in have heightened tensions with the state. Senior Catholic clergy were aware of the related dilemmas and avoided pushing their congregations to make a fundamental choice between church and state for fear of losing members. Gravely alarmed by the Pope's message, the Nazis forbade the circulation of the encyclical and confiscated printing presses from firms that continued to print copies. Catholic clergymen who referred to the encyclical in their sermons were arrested

Many Nazis, particularly Joseph Goebbels, seen here giving a speech to *Gauleiters* in Berlin, were fanatically hostile to the churches. Among the charges they levelled at priests were corruption and currency trafficking.

and incarcerated. Catholic laymen who dared to confess their faith in public by taking part in Corpus Christi processions or pilgrimages risked imprisonment or the loss of their jobs.

Unfortunately, *Mit brennender Sorge* remains an isolated example of dissent in the history of the Vatican's relations with the Nazi regime. This did not, of course, prevent Catholics of the calibre of Preysing from continuing to oppose the state. In most cases the motivation for this opposition was ecclesiastical-theological, yet the regime invariably saw itself as being under political and ideological attack. One of the most outstanding individuals to stand up for Christian values was the Bishop of Münster,

Clemens August Count von Galen. Here was a man with an imposing physical presence famed in his lifetime as "The Lion of Münster" for his public protests against Nazi crimes. It is surprising to discover, therefore, that after he was appointed bishop in September 1933 uniformed Nazis with swastika flags attended his consecration in October, when he took an oath of loyalty to the regime before Hermann Göring. Yet well before the outbreak of war Galen was beginning to come into conflict with the Nazis. In November 1936, for example, Nazi-appointed local officials ordered the removal of crucifixes as "symbols of super-stition" from schools in the Oldenburg district. This was a predominantly Catholic region and belonged to Galen's diocese of Münster. Galen ordered nine days of prayer for the retention of crucifixes in the churches, and the order was eventually rescinded on 4 November as a result of mass meetings that had taken place in the Cathedral Square in Münster.

GALEN ATTACKS THE GESTAPO
Numerous protests against Nazi lawlessness followed, culminating in three famous sermons preached in July and August 1941. The first of these sermons was delivered in the Lamberti Church on 13 July when Galen openly attacked the brutality of the Gestapo. His second sermon was preached in the Liebfrauenkirche on 20 July, and contained an unequivocal appeal for Christian duty in the face of religious persecution. In his third sermon on 3 August he famously denounced the Nazi "euthanasia" programme. In the course of his sermon he gave an account of the killing of defenceless mentally ill patients in the "euthanasia" institutions that had been set up in Warstein and Marienthal. Members of his congregation wept openly. Underground copies of the sermon circulated immediately throughout Germany

and were dropped from the air by Allied bomber aircraft.

Nothing illustrates the tension between church and state more vividly than the attempt by the Nazi regime to implement its euthanasia programme. On 1 September

> *Hitler issued an order to kill all persons with incurable diseases*

1939, the day that Poland was invaded, Hitler issued an order to kill all persons with incurable diseases. The idea of compulsory euthanasia had been in Hitler's mind for some time, but he had held back because of expected objections from the Catholic Church. The start of the war seemed the most propitious moment for inaugurating this radical eugenic programme. (The order was actually issued in October but backdated to 1 September.) After the war at the Nuremberg doctors' trial, Dr Karl Brandt, the Reichskommisar for Health, testified that: "In 1935 Hitler told the Reich Medical Leader, Dr Gerhard Wagner, that, if war came, he would take up and carry out this question of euthanasia because it was easier to do so in wartime when the church would not be able to put up the expected resistance." Such a programme would also provide much-needed hospital space for the wounded. Thus the euthanasia programme was in direct line of succession from the ster-ilization measures enacted in the early months of the regime.

Interestingly enough, as in the summer of 1941, so in the autumn of 1939, centrally organized and systematic killing was preceded by local initiatives. Between 29 September and 1 November 1939, SS units

The German Army on parade in the 1930s. Though religion was not overtly strong in the armed forces of the Third Reich, many senior officers were religious and viewed with distaste the Nazi attacks on the churches.

shot about 4000 mental patients in asylums in Poland. The first "euthanasia" installations opened in late December 1939 and early January 1940. As the so-called euthanasia action expanded, gassing in rooms designed as showers was introduced or lethal injections administered. It is estimated that between December 1939 and August 1941, at least 72,000 perished in institutions which operated under such fictitious names as the "Charitable Foundation for the Transportation of the Sick" and the "Charitable Foundation for Institutional Care".

Although corporately neither the churches nor the legal profession protested, as we have seen individual clergy did. Most notably Bishops Wurm and Meiser, and more famously Bishop Galen in his sermon delivered on 3 August 1941, revealed how the innocent sick were being killed while their families were misled by false death notices. The next of kin were notified that the patients had died of some ordinary disease and that their bodies had been cremated. Often they received warnings from the Secret Police not to demand explanations and not to "spread false rumours". Galen branded these deeds as criminal and demanded the prosecution for murder of those perpetrating them. Bishop Galen's disclosures struck a responsive chord, and copies of the sermon were distributed

Cardinal Galen of Münster, who organized an effective public protest against Nazi racial policies, specifically the euthanasia programme. Sent to Sachsenhausen after the July Bomb Plot, he was released in 1945.

throughout the Reich. His popularity made it impossible for the government to proceed against him, although some officials did propose that his "treasonable actions" warranted the death penalty. Goebbels feared that the "population of Münster could be regarded as lost during the war, if anything were to be done against the bishop, and in that fear one safely could include the whole of Westphalia".

GALEN'S COURAGE

The regime had underestimated the possibility of such a public reaction and the far-reaching nature of its impact. Shortly after Galen's sermon, the euthanasia programme was officially halted by a *Führerbefehl* (command from the Führer) of 24 August 1941 – although "wild euthanasia" killings through starvation or lethal medication continued. These public protests helped to form and consolidate public opinion, contributed to the general feeling of outrage, and led to the suspension of the euthanasia campaign. Thus the public conscience could still assert itself, even in 1941, when an issue affected the lives of Germans and their families. Post-war research has revealed that Galen was restrained from denouncing the persecution of the Jews by Jewish leaders in Münster, who feared reprisals. From 1936 Galen reckoned with arrest for his anti-Nazi sentiments, after 1941 with martyrdom. Nazi documents record the decision to hang Galen after "final victory". In fact, in March 1946 Pope Pius XII, who during the war had privately commended Galen for his courage, made him a cardinal, together with Preysing, his fellow bishop and cousin.

Apart from sporadic protests and despite individual acts of courage that resulted in persecution, the church's record in resisting Nazi atrocities is lamentable. Protestant leaders welcomed the Nazi Party because the

Hitler movement promised a national resurgence, the destruction of the Left, and the end of Weimar secularization. The innately conservative nature of Protestantism meant that they were unequivocally opposed to socialism, defensive against Catholicism, sceptical of democracy, and outspokenly nationalistic in their advocacy of German interests. Such conservatism had much in common with National

> ### By agreeing to the Concordat, the Pope had emasculated ecclesiastical opposition

Socialist aspirations. Throughout the life of the Third Reich, and not withstanding the initial expansion of the Pastors' Emergency League, out of 17,000 pastors across Germany, just 50 actually received substantial prison sentences for opposing the government – although around 400 Catholic priests and 35 Evangelical pastors were incarcerated for various periods in the Priests' Block at Dachau. The position of Catholicism during the early years of the Third Reich was more problematic than that of Protestantism. By agreeing to the Concordat with Hitler, the Pope had largely emasculated ecclesiastical resistance. In return for guarantees of complete religious freedom for Catholics in Germany, the Pope ordered his bishops to swear loyalty to the state, agreed to the dismantling of the Catholic trade unions, accepted the dissolution of the Centre Party and agreed to prohibit the clergy from political activity. For all these reasons, neither the Catholic nor the Protestant Church had the power or desire to incite their faithful to political resistance. It was left to a few courageous individual Christians, either

Karl Brandt, SS General and Reich Commissioner for Health, was responsible for the euthanasia programme that was halted by Galen. After the war he was tried by a US court for having approved inhuman experiments and hanged.

alone or aided by groups outside the church (such as the Kreisau Circle), to decide to take this path. Such "resistance" is all the more significant because it showed that such a path was compatible with Christian principles, in stark contrast to the silence of church leaders.

119

RESISTANCE AND GERMAN YOUTH

The youth groups that resisted the Nazi regime did so for a variety of reasons. Some politically challenged the regime, whereas others merely rejected the regimented lifestyle of the Hitler Youth.

The indoctrination of German youth was an important element in the Third Reich. To establish a Thousand Year Reich, Hitler aimed to educate all young people "in the spirit of National Socialism". With this aim

Hitler Youth boys at the 1935 Nuremberg Rally. When the Nazis came to power in 1933 the Hitler Youth organization had only 107,956 members; by the beginning of 1939 the number was a massive 7,500,000.

in mind, a number of youth organizations were set up to be run on National Socialist lines. From 1933, boys aged 10–14 years old joined the German Young People (*Deutsche Jungvolk* – DJ). When aged 14 they joined the Hitler Youth (*Hitlerjugend* – HJ). The head of the HJ, Baldur von Schirach, was given responsibility for coordinating all youth groups and bringing them under the control of the Party through the Hitler Youth organization (with the exception of a few Catholic religious youth organizations that had been tolerated under the terms of the Concordat). By 1935, 60 percent of all German youth belonged to the Hitler Youth,

Hitler with Hitler Youth members in Erfurt, Saxony. The Hitler Youth Law of December 1936 stated: "all German Young People ... will be educated in the Hitler Youth to serve the nation and the community."

the official state youth organization. Parents were put under enormous pressure to enroll their children, and questions were asked why some children had not joined up. In 1936 the HJ became a department of state and was officially recognized as representing all youth groups. Surprisingly, membership was not made compulsory until the Hitler Youth Law of 25 March 1939.

Baldur von Schirach, Hitler Youth leader, gives the Nazi salute at a *Hitlerjugend* rally in September 1938. Under Schirach the Hitler Youth became a state organization for indoctrination. Its motto was "Führer, command – we follow!"

At the age of 10 girls joined the League of Young Girls (*Jüngmädelbund* – JM), and at 14 they were expected to become members of the League of German Girls (*Bund Deutscher Mädel* – BDM). By 1936 the BDM had a membership of over two million girls. Although membership of the BDM remained optional until 1939, for a young girl to opt out of the organization was frowned upon. Girls in the BDM were taught to accept the role of mother and wife. At the age of 17, girls in the BDM could join the Faith and Beauty organization. Established in 1937, Faith and Beauty specialized in physical education, domestic science and preparation for marriage.

For the vast mass of German youth, however, Nazi propaganda offered youth comradeship and a pioneering role: the ideology of National Socialism represented the triumph of a rejuvenated Germany, liberated from outdated fallacies of bourgeois liberalism or Marxist class war. After all, it was to be this generation that would instil the Nazi *Weltanschauung* in their "national comrades", and lay the foundations for the New Order in Europe. As Hans Schemm, the leader of the Nazi Teachers' League, put it: "Those who have youth on their side control the future." In a

> ## "Your child belongs to us already ... Your descendants stand in the new camp"

celebrated speech on 6 November 1933 Hitler declared: "When an opponent says, 'I will not come over to your side,' I calmly say, 'Your child belongs to us already ... you will pass on. Your descendants, however, now stand in the new camp. In a short time they will know nothing else but this new community.'"

Although the growing regimentation and militarism of the youth organizations isolated some young Germans, the secret reports of the Social Democratic Party in exile (*Sopade*) in the 1930s tend to concede that the opportunities for participation, the comradeship and enthusiasm, together with the HJ's anti-intellectualism, generally attracted the support of young people. While some parents and teachers complained about the brutalizing effects of the *Hitlerjugend*, *Sopade* acknowledged that the contempt for the intellect cultivated by the HJ was a potent drawing card to youth itself: "The new generation has never had much use for education and reading. Now nothing is demanded of them; on the contrary,

knowledge is publicly condemned." Fired by nationalist rhetoric, Nazi education stressed the importance of "character building" and the value of "experience" (*Erlebnis*) to the

Baldur von Schirach (right) and Hitler at Nuremberg in September 1936. Schirach was from a middle class background and was fluent in English. An ardent Nazi, he reportedly read *Mein Kampf* in an evening.

development of the individual rather than the acquisition of "knowledge". Slogans like "youth must be led by youth" appealed to the desire of youth to be independent, and to challenge traditional authority figures in the name of the Nazi social "revolution".

To this end, concepts like *Volksgemeinschaft* ("Community of the People")

The German Young Folk (*Deutsches Jungvolk*), seen here, was made up of boys aged between 10 and 14. They took an oath to "devote all my energies and all my strength to the saviour of our country, Adolf Hitler."

provided a vehicle for the ambitions of a younger generation which had grown frustrated with a discredited establishment that had failed to solve Germany's national problems. The "battle for work" and the Nazi welfare schemes appeared to extend opportunities for social advancement, which had previously been denied to large sections of the youth population. Although the six months that students were obliged to undertake in the Labour Service was in reality a means of reducing overcrowding in the universities (and providing cheap labour) it served, nonetheless, to heighten an

awareness of the needs of the national community. Furthermore, the constant stress on achievement and competition within the youth movement (behind which lay the glorification of the heroic fighter) served to harness and channel young people's enthusiasm and project participation as a dynamic involvement. By 1939, 7.5 million young Germans were active participants of the Hitler Youth.

Nazi feature films, for example, depicted a German society in which class barriers were rapidly being broken down. Typical of the way in which this message was disseminated under the guise of film "entertainment" was the apparently innocuous comedy film *Der Stammbaum des Dr Pistorius* (*Dr Pistorius' Family Tree*), made in 1939. The film centres on the activities of the new German youth and the outmoded reactions of parents. A public official and his

> *Nazi films depicted a German society in which class barriers were being broken down*

wife have to learn to accept a daughter-in-law from a craftsman's family (cobbler). The father is heard to exclaim: "Youth today does not know what class consciousness is!" The Nazis had no qualms about criticizing social rank, provided such criticism was not too divisive. *Der Stammbaum des Dr Pistorius* ends with the same parents looking out at the Hitler Youth marching in the streets to the song: "Hearts are ready, fists are clenched, ready for the battles ahead," and their recognition coupled with a new respect that: "A new generation is coming – it is different from ours ... Youth today is

marching, it is stronger than we are." In this sense, youth gave a lead to the rest of the nation. Secret reports compiled by the SPD in exile suggested that: "the young people follow the instructions of the HJ and demand from their parents that they become good Nazis, that they give up Marxism, reactionism and contact with Jews. It is the young men who bring home enthusiasm for the Nazis. Old men no longer make any impression ... the secret of National Socialism is the secret of its youth."

THE NOTION OF COMMUNITY

German youth proved particularly receptive to the notion of a "national" or "people's" community. The assault on the individual, so characteristic of the regime, was directed primarily at youth with the intention of enveloping the individual at every stage of his or her development within a single organization by subjecting him to a planned course of indoctrination. Addressing the Nuremberg Party rally in September 1935, Hitler proclaimed: "What we look for from our German youth is different from what people wanted in the past. In our eyes the German youth of the future must be slim and slender, swift as the greyhound, tough as leather, and hard as Krupp steel. We must educate a new type of man so that our people is not ruined by the symptoms of degeneracy of our day." To this end the teaching profession represented one of the most politically reliable sections of the population, and from a very early stage was justly regarded by the NSDAP as a vanguard for its propaganda. Party control over the teaching profession was initially secured through the Führer Decree of 24 September 1935, which allowed political vetting by the Nazis for all Civil Service appointments. Teachers were also mobilized and controlled by means of their own professional association, the

Schirach with Hitler in 1938. When war broke out the youth leader fell from favour and was replaced by Arthur Axmann. Schirach became *Gauleiter* of Vienna, and after the war was sentenced to 20 years in prison for deporting Austrian Jews.

National Socialist Teachers' League (NSLB), which had been established as early as 1929. The NSLB provided political references for all appointments and promotions within the teaching profession, and generally attempted to maintain the political reliability of teachers through a process of ideological indoctrination. By 1937, the NSLB claimed a membership of over 95 percent of all teachers.

In *Mein Kampf* Hitler had laid great stress on organization, which included the organization of leisure time as well. Indoctrination in schools was therefore reinforced by the "new comradeship" of the *Hitlerjugend* and its female counterpart, the League of German Girls. Writing in 1937, the historian Stephen Roberts, who had spent over a year in Germany observing the youth system, referred to the "triumph of Nazi propaganda over teaching", and went on to comment:

"Again and again in Germany, even in Catholic Bavaria and the Black Forest, I found cases of children whose Roman

Catholic parents tried to keep them in the few struggling Church societies that still exist for children. In every case the children wanted to join the *Hitlerjugend* ... To be outside Hitler's organization was the worst form of punishment. The resultant worship was too distressing. Their attitude of mind is absolutely uncritical. They do not see in Hitler a statesman with good and bad points; to them he is more than a demigod ... It is this utter lack of any objective or critical attitude on the part of youth, even with the university students, that made me fear most for the future of Germany. They are nothing but vessels for State propaganda."

Such contemporary impressions were certainly encouraged by the German government. However, the belief that the Hitler Youth had successfully mobilized all young people is clearly an exaggeration.

"Though their minds were deliberately poisoned, their regular schooling interrupted ... the boys and the girls ... seemed immensely happy, filled with a zest for the life of a Hitler Youth." (The author William Shirer)

There is considerable evidence to suggest that by the late 1930s the regimental nature of the Hitler Youth was alienating some young people, who were forming independent gangs. Various youth groups did, in fact, attempt to resist the aspects of the regimental nature of the HJ. The two most documented

> ## The "Swing Youth" tended to be the offspring of the urban middle class

"non-conformist" groups who rejected the Hitler Youth, though for different reasons, were the "Swing Youth" (*Swingjugend*) and the "Edelweiss Pirates" (*Edelweisspiraten*).

The "Swing Youth" were certainly not anti-fascist. They tended to be the offspring of the urban middle class, with the money and status to reject *völkische* music and listen instead to jazz and swing music, which the authorities labelled as American-influenced *Unkultur* (degeneracy) and later banned. The "Swingers" showed no interest in political activities, preferring to flaunt an unconventional lifestyle based on pleasurable consumption – the very antithesis of the soldierly ideal of the Hitler Youth movement. The "Swingers'" leisure time was to "hang-out" in bars and to dance uninhibitedly to swing music. They cultivated a special appearance that consisted of long hair, checkered jackets and umbrellas slung over their arms. In addition, they greeted one another with English nicknames. The HJ reports were concerned less with what was invariably referred to as "negro music" but with sexual promiscuity, lack of parental discipline and a general cult of "sleaziness" that surrounded these groups. The "Swing Youth" cultivated a somewhat élitist culture that rejected the strident nationalism of the Hitler Youth but was nonetheless politically indifferent to National Socialism. The Nazis for their part viewed them as an irritant. Heinrich Himmler found them particularly irritating, and in a letter written in January 1942 to Reinhard Heydrich, the Chief of the Security Police and the Security Service, the *Reichsführer-SS* demanded that all the ringleaders be transported to concentration camps. In fact, most of the ringleaders had already been arrested and imprisoned by October 1940.

The "Edelweiss" group, on the other hand, represented a more serious challenge to the social conformity that the Hitler Youth attempted to instil. Generally known as the "Edelweiss Pirates", they were a loose amalgamation of subgroups with a variety of names. For example, in 1937 a court in Cologne identified constellations of teenagers calling themselves "Navajos". In 1939 the Essen Gestapo discovered even more youths calling themselves "Edelweiss Pirates". As a result, the Gestapo and the judiciary tended to persecute dissenting

> ## The "Edelweiss" group, on the other hand, represented a more serious challenge

groups of youth under the umbrella term "Edelweiss Pirates". The origin of the term has not been definitely determined. It was probably coined by the persecuting authorities, who recognized that some of the youths brought before them wore an edelweiss badge. Prior to this, the Nazi

Hess (left), Hitler (centre) and Schirach (right) at a youth rally. "These young people learn nothing else but to think as Germans and to act as Germans; these boys join our organization at the age of 10 and get a breath of fresh air." (Hitler)

authorities used the term "Kittelbach Pirates", which can be traced back to a hiking club of the same name that was founded in Düsseldorf in 1925 and was so named after a small river. This hiking club was initially sympathetic to the Nazis. However, when it was "coordinated" into the Hitler Youth organization in 1933, some members rebelled and insisted on their own independence. As an outlawed club, it rapidly gained a reputation among discontented youth, as would the "Edelweiss Pirates" later, for being attractively "dangerous" and Bohemian.

THE "EDELWEISS PIRATES"

The first "Edelweiss Pirates" sprang up spontaneously towards the end of the 1930s in the Rhenish-Westphalian industrial area. In contrast to "Swing Youth", the "Edelweiss Pirates" were a working class phenomenon. It is estimated, for example, that there were several thousand youths who were considered by the Nazi authorities to be "Edelweiss Pirates". Consisting mainly of young people between the ages of 14 and 18, individual groups were closely associated with different regions but identifiable by a common style of dress (short pants and loudly checked shirts), with their death's head rings, their own edelweiss insignia on their lapels and a general oppositional attitude towards what they saw as the increasingly paramilitary obligations of the Hitler Youth. Prior to the outbreak of war, nearly a quarter of the members of the HJ in the Rhineland town of Krefeld were believed to belong to the "Edelweiss" group, whose main purpose was to meet in secret, discuss events, share information and reaffirm their largely religious objections to the Nazi regime. Another significant contribution to the group's attractiveness was that, in contrast to the Hitler Youth, the sexes were not separated (even in the HJ this was not always the reality, since, for example, the League of German Girls was nicknamed the

"League of German Mattresses"). The fact that young people could meet in these diverse groups, together with the danger of being outlawed, only added to its appeal. Although the "Edelweiss Pirates" rejected the authoritarian and hierarchical lifestyle of the Nazis, their non-conformist behaviour tended to be restricted to petty provocation, not political opposition. The movement was

Hitler meets a group of young girls in 1937. In general the Nazi attitude towards women was negative: they were expected to be good house-keepers and produce future generations of soldiers for the Third Reich.

motivated less by ideological anti-Nazi beliefs than by a spontaneous and emotional rejection of repressive conditions of everyday life found in the Third Reich. Fourteen- to eighteen-year-olds could hardly be expected to pose a serious political threat, or indeed offer a political alternative to National Socialism. There were exceptions to this rule, and the actions of the Essen "Gallivanters" should be mentioned. They painted the slogan "Down with Hitler" on the houses of the district of Segeroth and distributed subversive literature. There was also the "resistance" activities of the Düsseldorff "Edelweiss Pirates", who

worked together with cells from the German Communist resistance. In the bombed-out ruins of the working class district of Ehrenfeld in Cologne in 1944, there was a group of "Edelweiss Pirates", German deserters and escaped foreign workers who maintained loose contact with the German Communist Party and carried out more than a dozen assassinations of Nazi functionaries. Thirteen members of the group, including three "Edelweiss Pirates" who had not yet reached the age of majority, were publicly hanged by the Gestapo on 10 November 1944. It has to be stressed that these

Members of the *Bund Deutscher Mädel* (League of German Girls), the girls' organization of the Hitler Youth. Many young German females were attracted to this movement, believing it to be part of a new era.

represent rare exceptions, though. By and large the "Edelweiss Pirates" represent a very small group of youths who rebelled against regimented leisure and who remained unimpressed by the propaganda eulogizing a racial "people's community". For the most part, their non-conformist activities consisted of wearing their own

131

Hitler Youth physical fitness, weapons drills and general outdoor activities were major attractions to German youth in the 1930s. These girls are members of the Nazi German Women's Youth Movement, 1935.

clothing and planned altercations with the paramilitary patrols of the Hitler Youth. Nevertheless, the Reich Youth Leadership and the Gestapo took these skirmishes – and indeed any form of hostility to the HJ –

extremely seriously. "Edelweiss Pirates" and youth gangs in general who were caught by the police could expect to be dealt with severely by the state. They would be handed over to the Gestapo and the Nazi justice system and severely punished.

THE "LEIPZIG HOUND PACKS"

The most significant gang, or "wild cliques" as they were invariably referred to by the Gestapo, was the "Leipzig Hound Packs", which sprang up in the working suburbs of Leipzig in 1937. These appear to have been spontaneous meetings of youths of both sexes who came from the same area, wore the same clothes, and greeted one another with the Russian Youth Pioneers' bellowing call. Most of their activities consisted of non-conformist behaviour – meeting in bars and arranging weekend trips – in contrast to the planned and regimentalized leisure organized by the HJ. They decisively rejected the Hitler Youth, and Gestapo files suggest that pitched battles frequently erupted between the two sets of youth. The "Leipzig Hounds" also regularly listened to Radio Moscow, and some sections within the "pack" attempted to form a counter-organization to the Hitler Youth along communist lines. In 1938 it has been estimated that the "Leipzig Hound Packs" could boast 1500 members. In January 1940, some of its leaders were sentenced by the People's Court and the State Court of Dresden to long years of imprisonment.

In contrast to the "Swing Youth", and to some extent the "Edelweiss Pirates", were three small political groups that independently and without knowledge of each other had emerged in Hamburg, Munich and Vienna in 1941. These groups became known as the "Gangs of Four" because each group was comprised of four male youths between the ages of 16 and 18, and each had

an outstandingly precocious leader: Helmut Hübener in Hamburg, Walter Klingenbeck in Munich and Josef Landgraf in Vienna. The members of all three groups came from Christian families of the lower middle class, and all three groups were motivated to political resistance because of their own disillusioned experiences of National Socialism. None of the groups had constructed alternative political programmes; instead they were concerned only with the overthrow of the regime and an Allied victory. From the summer of 1941 until February 1942, Hübener and three friends distributed leaflets that they had collated from forbidden BBC radio news reports. Hübener and two of his friends, Karl-Heinz Schnibbe and Rudi Wobbe, were members of the Hamburg Mormon congregation that had established relatively cordial links with

> *Hübener and three friends distributed leaflets that they had collated*

the National Socialists. The fourth member, Gerhard Düwer, was persuaded to join the group at the beginning of 1942. A total of 60 leaflets were circulated, all contrasting "official" *Wehrmacht* reports of the war with BBC bulletins and attacking Nazi social policy and lampooning individual Nazi leaders. At the beginning of February 1942, Hübener was betrayed by a fellow worker who had witnessed him trying unsuccessfully to persuade an apprentice to translate a flyer into French for distribution among the foreign workers. On 11 August 1942, Hübener was sentenced to death by the People's Court in Berlin for high treason. His three co-defendants, Schnibbe, Wobbe and Düwer, received prison sentences of between four to 10 years. Hübener was decapitated in Berlin-Plötzensee on 27 October 1942.

Walter Klingenbeck, a Catholic mechanic in Munich, suffered the same fate. Klingenbeck continued to listen to the German-language service of the BBC and Vatican Radio long after they were outlawed in September 1939. He was later joined by two friends, Hans Haberl and Daniel von Recklinghausen. In the summer of 1941 he and his friends took up the BBC's appeal and daubed more than 40 buildings with "V-for-

> ## *All three were arrested in January 1942 and sentenced to death by the People's Court*

victory" signs as symbols of a victory for the Western Allies. Klingenbeck was also preparing to set up his own clandestine anti-Nazi radio propaganda station and was about to distribute leaflets claiming: " Hitler Cannot Win the War – He Can Only Prolong It!". All three were arrested in January 1942 and sentenced to death by the People's Court on 24 September. A fourth youth who was only marginally implicated was handed down an eight-year sentence. Although Haberl's and von Recklinghausen's sentences were commuted to eight years' imprisonment on appeal, Klingenbeck was executed in Munich-Stadlheim on 5 August 1943.

The third "Gangs of Four" was led by Viennese high school student Josef Landgraf. He was joined by schoolmates Ludwig Igalffy, Friedrich Fexer and Anton Brunner. Landgraf and his group listened to forbidden foreign broadcasts and transcribed what

they had heard in leaflets that contradicted German war propaganda. They also adopted the "V-campaign" advocated by the BBC from London. Landgraf was extraordinarily productive in the short space of time before

he was denounced, producing on his father's typewriter over 140 flyers, leaflets and stickers. One of which proclaimed: "The V-army's sole aim is the liberation from Hitler and his war." Landgraf and Brunner were

Reichsführer-SS **Heinrich Himmler (second from left) was incensed by the activities of the dissident "Edelweiss Pirates", and ordered his deputy Reinhard Heydrich (second from right) to wipe them out.**

Red Army troops advancing on the Eastern Front. Thousands of Hitler Youth members ended up in the *Wehrmacht* fighting the Soviets in Hitler's crusade against Bolshevism. Most went willingly – to the great disappointment of anti-Hitler groups.

sentenced to death by the People's Court on 23 August 1942. The two other defendants were given eight and six years' imprisonment respectively. One year later, Landgraf's sentence was commuted to seven years' imprisonment and Brunner's sentence was reduced to five years' imprisonment. The social background of all three groups was petty bourgeois. While they were determined to resist National Socialism and bring the war to an end, they were not ideologically motivated, although it is fair to say that they had a strong affinity with the Western Allies and a basic Christian orientation. In fact, they possessed similar characteristics to perhaps the most famous youth resistance group – the "White Rose".

The group named "White Rose" became the symbol of resistance based on youthful idealism. It was a group consisting of students and friends from Munich, and its resistance actions consisted mainly of the composition and dissemination of six anti-Nazi leaflets between June 1942 and February 1943, and ended with the spectacular action of the Scholls at Munich University on 18 February 1943. The group of friends that made up the "White Rose" evolved slowly over a period of time. Medical students Hans Scholl (aged 24) and Alexander Schmorell (25) were the core of the group; Sophie Scholl (21), Christopher Probts (23), Willi Graf (25) and Professor Kurt Huber (49) gradually became actively involved in the group's activities over a period of time. All the young students came from comfortable, conservative-bourgeois, Christian-orientated families. They were well educated and highly articulate. Hans

> *Hans and Sophie Scholl grew up with three other children in a liberal household*

and Sophie Scholl grew up with three other children in a liberal Protestant household. They were children of an anti-Nazi small-town Bürgermeister in Swabia who was himself in trouble in 1942 for calling Hitler a "scourge from God". Schmorell was the son of a Munich doctor, who had married the daughter of an Orthodox priest in Russia in 1915. As a result, Schmorell could speak Russian fluently and was greatly influenced by Russian culture. Probts came from a social environment that was similar that of Schmorell's, whom he knew from secondary school. His father was an independently wealthy private scholar and connoisseur. Probts was sent to the German equivalent of an English public school, and he married at a young age and had three children. Willi Graf was the son of a wine wholesaler from

the Rhineland and he grew up in a staunchly Catholic household. Graf refused to join the Hitler Youth on religious, as opposed to political, grounds. Like Schmorell, he chose to remain in the banned *Bündische Jugend* (Youth League). Both were jailed for continuing to be associated with these

On the Eastern Front many Hitler Youth members fought, in Hitler's words, "magnificently and with incredible bravery … the youngsters who come from the Hitler Youth are fanatical fighters". Like these, they also died in their thousands.

A German prisoner at Stalingrad. A "White Rose" pamphlet said of the defeat: "The genial strategy of the World War I corporal has senselessly and irresponsibly driven 330,000 German men to death and ruin. Führer, we thank you!"

outlawed youth organizations. Hans Scholl by contrast had joined the *Hitlerjugend* (much to his father's disapproval) and had risen to the rank of squad leader, until a fistfight with a higher-ranking leader ended

> **Sophie Scholl rose to be a squad leader in the League of German Girls**

his Hitler Youth career. Following a visit to the Nuremberg Party Rally in 1935, he became disillusioned with its militaristic narrow-mindedness, after which he too joined the *Bündische Jugend* and was also jailed. Sophie Scholl rose to be a squad leader in the League of German Girls before she too turned against it.

THE "WHITE ROSE"

There remains a mystery surrounding the origin of the name "White Rose" under which the leaflets were distributed. The accepted version is that it was taken from a novel of the same name (*Die Weisse Rose*) written by a German under the pseudonym of B. Traven. The novel was about a Mexican farm which had escaped the corruptions of civilization. Under interrogation by the Gestapo, however, Hans Scholl claimed that the name had been chosen arbitrarily but that it was possible that he took it after reading the Spanish romance *La Rosa Blanca* by Clemens von Brentano. Scholl told the Gestapo that he was less concerned with the

origin of the name "White Rose" than with its potential effectiveness in successful propaganda distribution.

The group of friends that made up the "White Rose" evolved slowly. The group only accepted persons who had proven their trustworthiness. The main criterion for membership was not necessarily a political rejection of National Socialism, but rather a moral one and the affirmation of those intellectual, cultural and religious values that Nazism set out to destroy. What united the group together was its shared interest in art,

German prisoners after the fall of Stalingrad. Hans Scholl served for a while as an orderly on the Eastern Front, and he was horrified at what he heard and saw. It made him determined to campaign for the removal of Hitler.

music and literature. It was this interest that drew them to Professor Kurt Huber, a musicologist and philosopher at Munich University. Huber's influence is palpable. Hans and Sophie Scholl and their friends began attending his lectures during the summer of 1942, in which he openly discussed questions and thinkers that had been declared taboo. Between 27 June and 12 July 1942, the group's first four leaflets appeared in Munich in the mailboxes of a selected intellectual élite. Entitled *Leaflets of the White Rose*, they called for passive resistance against the regime. The authors were Hans Scholl and Alexander Schmorell. The leaflets were written in high-flown language, widely spiced with literary references, and they appealed to Christian values. The *First Leaflet* began: "It is certain that today every honest German is ashamed of his government. Who among us has any conception of the dimensions of shame that will befall us and our children when one day the veil has fallen from our eyes and the most horrible of crimes – crimes that infinitely outdistance every other human measure – reach the light of day?" The *Second Leaflet* referred to "three hundred thousand Jews being murdered in Poland" (evidence that the treatment of Jews was known in Germany), and the *Third Leaflet* called for sabotage: "SABOTAGE in armaments plants and war industries, SABOTAGE at all gatherings, rallies, public ceremonies and organizations of the National Socialist Party ... Do not contribute to the collections of metal, textiles and the like. Try to convince all your acquaintances ... of the senselessness of continuing, of the hopelessness of this War."

LINKS WITH OTHER GROUPS

From July until November 1942, Hans Scholl, Schmorell and Graf were sent with their Student Company to the southern front in Russia as medical orderlies. The experience had a profound impact on them, and inspired by their impressions of Russia and horrified by the senseless atrocities of the war, they intensified their resistance activities after their return in November. They began establishing links with a network of resistance circles in other university cities. Through Falk Harnack, the students attempted to make contact with individuals and groups coordinating resistance from Berlin, including the Red Orchestra and the Bonhöffer brothers.

Early in January 1943 Hans Scholl drafted the *Fifth Leaflet – A Call to All Germans* – which Huber revised. This was different from previous leaflets, in terms of both content and style. It condemned "Prussian militarism" and "Nazi barbarism" and called for a "federal"

> ## The Scholls always posted a leaflet to themselves to deceive Gestapo surveillance

Germany based on "freedom of speech, freedom of belief, protection of the individual against the arbitrary action of criminal power – these are the foundations of a new Europe." This was decidedly more political, and concrete plans for a post-war Germany are presented. Several thousand of these leaflets were distributed by hand or by post in Munich and Augsburg, while others were taken (or posted) to Ulm, Stuttgart, Frankfurt, Bonn, Karlsruhe, Salzburg, Linz and Vienna, so as to give the impression that the movement had more than one centre. The Scholls always posted a leaflet to themselves to ensure that they were deceiving Gestapo surveillance. On 13 January, to mark the 470th anniversary of the university, the Munich *Gauleiter* Paul Giesler made a highly provocative speech to a large student gathering. He informed the women that, instead of hanging around as students, they should be presenting sons to the Führer. This remark evoked a wave of indignation that electrified the entire student body and led to a violent confrontation with the police. When the Sixth Army's defeat at Stalingrad became known after 3 February, Willi Graf, Alexander Schmorell and Hans Scholl on several occasions painted slogans like "Freedom", "Down with Hitler" and "Hitler Mass Murderer" on university buildings and in central Munich. The obvious change of mood that took hold of the public caused the "White Rose" friends to risk these more daring activities of graffiti, in order reach the masses. Sensing that this represented a real turning point in the war, they decided to produce a new leaflet specif-

ically addressed to students. Huber wrote it for them, comparing 1943 with 1813 and calling for the liberation of Europe from the slavery of National Socialism. Some 3000 copies were produced but few were distributed by post. Instead, the Scholls decided to take the leaflets to the university and distribute them among the students. But then Hans and Sophie Scholl did something

Munich University, where on the morning of 18 February 1943 the Scholls distributed "White Rose" pamphlets. Unsurprisingly, they were caught and handed over to the Gestapo – it is sad to report that many students cheered their arrest.

Sophie Scholl, one of the leading members of the "White Rose" student group. In court before Roland Freisler she accused those present of agreeing with what the group had stood for but being afraid to do anything about it.

deposited several more stacks, and then up to the third floor, where Sophie tossed the remainder of the leaflets over the balcony. The university porter, Jakob Schmid, saw the leaflets cascading down, grabbed them and hauled them off to the Rector, an SS *Oberführer* (brigadier-general). Some of the students are said to have cheered their arrest.

Concerned that events might escalate even further, Roland Freisler, the fanatical President of the People's Court, was summoned by the Gestapo to Munich on 22 February. After a trial lasting three and a half hours, the two Scholls and Probts were sentenced to death. Sophie had told Freisler: "You know as well as we do that the war is lost. Why are you too cowardly to admit it?" Shortly before Hans' execution, his sister Inge visited him in prison. After bidding each other farewell, he turned and wrote on his white cell wall. The words on the wall were a quotation from Goethe: "Remain yourself in spite of all the mighty do" (*Allen Gewalten zum Trotz sich erhalten*). The sentences were carried out by guillotine three hours later.

RETRIBUTION

The Gestapo had no trouble locating the rest of the group. In the Scholls' bedrooms they had found the addresses and telephone numbers they needed (the Scholls had refused to name collaborators, even though Sophie endured a 17-hour interrogation). The second trial against the "White Rose" took place on 19 April 1943 and lasted for 14 hours as the defendants, in contrast to the first trial, insisted on their right to a defence. Of the 14 defendants, Willi Graf, Kurt Huber and Alexander Schmorell received the death sentence; Huber and Schmorell were executed on 13 July, Graf on 12 October. The rest received sentences of imprisonment ranging from six months to 10 years. A third trial in conjunction with the "White Rose"

that will always remain a mystery. On the morning of 18 February, they went to the university with a suitcase and a briefcase containing copies of the *Sixth Leaflet* and a few copies of the *Fifth*. The Scholls placed stacks of leaflets in front of the closed auditoriums and in the corridors. They then went up to the second floor, where they took place against Harold Dohrn, Manfred Eickemeyer, Wilhelm Geyer and Joseph Söhngen in Munich on 13 July 1943. Only Söhngen was actually convicted, and he was given a six-month prison sentence; the others were acquitted.

Although the core of the "White Rose" resistance group was silenced, their courageous deeds became known beyond Munich. Thomas Mann, for example, honoured them on the BBC in June 1943. In Hamburg a few groups similar to the one created by the Scholls already existed and

> ## *The British dropped leaflets on Germany that drew attention to the "White Rose" group*

comprised about 50 people. When they heard what had happened in Munich, they duplicated and distributed some of the "White Rose" leaflets with an addendum, *Their Spirit Lives On*. Thirty people were arrested for organizing a collection in aid of Kurt Huber's widow. A trial before the People's Court took place in Donauwörth on 13 October 1944, and Hans Leipelt, who took the money to Munich, was sentenced to death and guillotined on 29 January 1945. The British also dropped several thousand leaflets over Germany that drew attention to the resistance of the "White Rose" group. While it cannot be claimed that they influenced the course of the war – or indeed hastened the end of National Socialism – their activities and the manner of their resistance provided an example for those in the post-war period of reconstruction who sought the existence of "another" Germany. "White Rose's" legacy was, and still is, instrumental for a number of political and

religious movements. In Germany today their memory is celebrated in a permanent institution: The White Rose Foundation.

Hans Scholl. Both he and his sister, together with Christoph Probts, were found guilty of treason and immediately after the trial were taken to Stadelheim prison. There, in the courtyard, all three were guillotined.

MILITARY RESISTANCE AND ASSASSINATION ATTEMPTS

Of all the groups that offered resistance to Hitler, the army was in the best position to topple the Führer. And when the tide of war turned against Germany, some officers made attempts on his life.

Under the ubiquitous Nazi system of terror and coercion, it would be inconceivable that resistance among disparate groups of disaffected German youth could have toppled the regime. The only section of German

Hitler with members of the Waffen-SS. The SS was originally created to protect the Führer, and would-be army assassins found it increasingly difficult to get past the constant SS bodyguard that surrounded Hitler wherever he went.

society that could realistically have challenged the omnipresence of the Gestapo and the SS was the armed forces. It is to the military resistance that I must now finally turn.

German soldiers surrender to Red Army members on the Eastern Front. The severe losses experienced by the army in Russia undoubtedly contributed to the growing disenchantment felt by its members as the war dragged on.

The Treaty of Versailles, which the subsequent Weimar Republic was forced to accept after the military defeat and the collapse of Wilhelmine Germany in 1919, reduced the armed forces of the German Reich to a professional army, now called the *Reichswehr*, of 100,000 men. Moreover, in order to prevent a gradual increase in size through the training of reservists, the Treaty further forbade Germany universal conscription. The character of the *Reichswehr* was thus largely composed of long-term volunteers. Therefore, while the army remained loyal to the Weimar Republic, the higher-ranking officer corps, which had received its professional training in the Imperial Army, felt bitter about military defeat and alienated from this new army. Despite the fact that it was obliged to maintain political neutrality, the *Reichswehr* remained sympathetic to any political movement in Germany that pledged itself to revise Versailles and the treaty's military limitations.

It is no surprise, therefore, to discover that the *Reichswehr* welcomed Hitler as a champion of its cause: from rearmament to the restoration of Germany as a great political and military power. The army was impressed by the importance that the Nazis attached to everything military and by ceremonies such as the "Day of Potsdam" (21 March 1933), when the Reich President Paul von Hindenburg, the hero of Tannenberg, shook the hand of Chancellor Hitler, World War I corporal, publicly entrusting him with the responsibility for the fate of the nation. The *Reichswehr* kept a supportive low profile while Hitler eliminated parliamentary

> ## Hitler acted swiftly and ordered the purge of the leadership of the SA

democracy and established in its place the one-party state.

In June 1934, Hitler won the favour of the General Staff by purging the SA (*Sturmabteilung* or Storm Troopers), the Nazi paramilitaries, in the "Night of the Long Knives". Because of its size and conservative nature, the *Reichswehr* was concerned about the growing size of the SA and the ambitions of its leader, Ernst Röhm. A group of leading generals had demanded that Hitler discipline the SA and Röhm. Recognizing that conservative groups were still politically important because they retained Hindenburg's support, Hitler acted swiftly and ordered the purge of the leadership of the SA. On 30 June, the SA was brutally eliminated. Röhm was arrested and two days later was shot. In all, about 180 Nazis associated with the SA were executed. These included SA leaders such as Karl Ernst

and Edmund Hennes. Others were also murdered, including two former generals of the *Reichswehr*, ex-Chancellor Kurt von Schleicher and Ferdinand von Bredow.

The "Night of the Long Knives" was a vital step for Hitler in the consolidation of his own power within the Party, and it resulted in a closer alliance between the Nazi state and the *Reichswehr*. Without the *Reichswehr*'s logistical support (SS squads which carried out the executions were provided with *Reichswehr* transport for the purpose), Hitler's murderous action against the SA leadership would not have been possible. The simultaneous upgrading of the SS as an autonomous élite unit under Himmler did not, apparently, cause army officers the same level of concern.

THE NEW ARMY OATH

Just over a month after the culling of the SA leadership, Hitler decided to consolidate his position even further. Until July 1934, the oath of allegiance taken by the *Reichswehr* was as follows:

"I swear by God this holy oath that I will serve my people and Fatherland at all times as a worthy soldier and will be ready at any time to risk my life for this oath."

On 2 August 1934, the day of Hindenburg's death and the day on which Hitler assumed the office of President of the Reich and Supreme Commander of the Armed Forces, the oath was changed to:

"I swear by God this holy oath that I will render unconditional obedience to the Führer of the German Reich and People, Adolf Hitler, the Supreme Commander of the Armed Forces, and as a worthy soldier I will be ready at all times to risk my life for this oath."

In changing the oath in this manner Hitler had established a binding obligation from the *Reichswehr* to him personally. On

The marriage of Karl Ernst, senior official in the SA, in September 1933. Immediately behind the happy couple stand Ernst Röhm, SA leader (left), and Hermann Göring (right). Röhm was killed in the "Night of the Long Knives".

19 August, a plebiscite produced a result of 89.9 percent support for uniting the offices of head of state and head of government in Hitler's person.

A new relationship between Hitler and the *Reichswehr* had been established as a result of the death of Hindenburg and the culling of the SA. Moreover, the political situation appeared extremely promising. On 13 January 1935, more than 90 percent of the population of the Saar supported incorporation into the German Reich, and on 16 March military conscription was announced with the aim of building an army of 36 divisions. The hated Versailles restrictions were being removed, apparently without any damaging repercussions for Germany. Moreover, the 1936 Olympic Games held in Berlin proved a huge propaganda coup for Nazi Germany. These developments, together with the burgeoning arms build-up, opened up excellent opportunities for officers. They were also getting promotions; the 44 generals of 1932 had become 261 by the end of 1938.

THE FIRST VOICES OF DISSENT

The army had recovered its honoured position on the national stage, symbolized by the importance attached in the Third Reich to military values, pomp and ceremony. While the generals were, on the whole, well satisfied with events, the end of 1937 and the beginning of 1938 witnessed the coalescence of the first circles of officers who began to believe that Hitler had to be stopped. There were two reasons for this: Hitler's domestic manoeuvres, and what was seen as a reckless expansionist foreign policy.

There was concern among some of the generals when, on 5 November 1937, they were informed of Hitler's intention to invade Czechoslovakia. The War Minister, Field Marshal von Blomberg, and Supreme Commander of the Armed Forces, Colonel

Heinrich Himmler, head of the SS. The emasculation of the SA during the "Night of the Long Knives" was a turning point in the SS's fortunes. But in 1934 the army did not view the bespectacled Himmler and his SS as a threat.

removed). These events triggered a dramatic turning point that eventually led to Hitler assuming control of the armed forces (known as the *Wehrmacht* and newly created in 1935 from the army, navy and air force), and in the process emasculating the army as an independent force. Von Blomberg had to resign on 4 February 1938 when it came to light that he had married an ex-prostitute, and the Gestapo fabricated evidence in order to discredit von Fritsch as

> ## The Gestapo fabricated evidence in order to discredit von Fritsch

a homosexual. By mid-1938, Hitler had sufficiently weakened potential opposition from "conservative" generals and could now initiate an expansionist foreign policy in pursuit of German hegemony.

Outraged at these intrigues (especially against von Fritsch), several officers decided to end the alliance between themselves and the Nazi movement. The Chief of the General Staff, General Beck, was the first to warn against the invasion of Czechoslovakia. Ludwig Beck was born in 1880, the son of a distinguished civil engineer in Hesse. Continuing a family tradition that had only been interrupted by his father, he became an officer in the army, being promoted to the General Staff in 1911. Beck was a highly gifted soldier, but was by

General von Fritsch, expressed their reservations and were eventually relieved of their positions. Within weeks of the meeting (recorded in the so-called Hossbach memorandum), the army had set out a strategic plan for an offensive against Czechoslovakia, and a few months later a bloodless purge removed the remnants of the conservative old guard (16 generals were no means a blinkered militarist. He believed that the moral basis of his profession was its function of guaranteeing the security of the nation. He recognized the primacy of the political sphere to govern. However, he also considered it good practice for those in positions of political responsibility in war-like situations to listen to the arguments of the military experts. In May 1938, when Hitler announced to his generals that he had "decided irreversibly" to invade Czechoslovakia at the next propitious

opportunity, Beck was the first to warn against this move, fearing that it might result in incalculable military consequences. Beck had already disapproved of marching into Austria in March, and he feared that further aggression would force Britain and France to

SA leader Ernst Röhm in his study. He regarded his SA as the true army of Nazi Germany, a view that both alarmed and dismayed the army's High Command. His murder in June 1934 earned Hitler the army's gratitude.

declare war in support of Czechoslovakia. Having failed to persuade von Fritsch's successor, General von Brauchitsch, to support a collective act of subordination on the part of the generals, he resigned from his post in August 1938.

Beck now became the central figure in a small group of reliable officers (including his successor, General Halder) that began to conspire seriously against Hitler. Although it would have been impossible to have persuaded the majority of the General Staff into collective action against Hitler, the notion of a Putsch no longer seemed improbable. Beck and Halder had won over officers such as Erwin von Witzleben, the Commanding General in the Third Army's Corps District III (Berlin), and Count Brockdorff-Ahlefeldt, the Commander of the Potsdam Garrison.

There was also Hans Oster of the *Abwehr* (Counterintelligence), who had exposed the defamatory campaign carried out against Fritsch. His attempts, supported by Beck and Admiral Canaris, Chief of Counterintelligence, to persuade Britain to adopt a firmer stand against Hitler regarding the Sudetenland question, had been undermined by the Munich settlement.

This small military coalescence had also made contact with the civilian resistance surrounding the "Goerdeler Circle". Beck's rare ability, for a soldier, to meet civilians (and politicians) on a common intellectual plane brought him into contact with Carl Goerdeler, arguably the most outstanding civilian conservative to oppose Hitler.

CARL GOERDELER

Carl Goerdeler was born in 1884 in West Prussia, and was brought up in a home dominated by the traditional Bismarckian politics of piety and probity. In 1899, when he was 15, his father, who had been a district judge in the West Prussian town of Marienweder, was elected a conservative deputy in the Prussian Diet. From 1920 to 1930 Carl Goerdeler was Deputy Mayor of Königsberg. He joined the German National People's Party (DNVP) in 1922 and was elected to its council, but disapproved of Alfred Hugenberg's opposition to Chancellor Heinrich Brüning and resigned in

> **Beck now became a central figure in a small group of reliable officers**

1931. From 1930 to 1937 he was Mayor of Leipzig. In addition, he was Price Commissioner under Brüning (who sacked him) and Hitler, who re-appointed him in November 1934. Hitler thought highly of him, and in fact paid considerable attention to his advice about local government reform.

Leipzig was one of the few German cities which had the same Bürgermeister at the end of 1933 as it did at the beginning, although Goerdeler refused in October an invitation from Hitler to join the Nazi Party. Goerdeler remained initially ambivalent in his attitudes towards the Nazis. For example, he supported the Enabling Act of March 1933 which authorized Hitler to pass laws for four years without reference to the *Reichstag*. He also welcomed Hitler's audacious revisions of the Versailles Treaty. Yet he refused to allow the swastika flag to fly over Leipzig's City Hall, and went out of his way to protect Jewish shopkeepers from Nazi thuggery not sanctioned by law. Goerdeler eventually came to oppose the Nazis after he had time to analyze them. Precisely because of his conservative Christian background, he totally rejected their exaggerated nationalism, racism and lack of respect for the established order. When the Nazis tore down the monument erected for the Jewish composer Felix Mendelssohn-Bartholdy in front of Leipzig's *Gewandhaus* (Cloth Hall) in late 1936, he resigned his office.

His biographer, Gerhard Ritter, wrote: "Carl Goerdeler as little as most other Germans fathomed from the beginning the full demonic nature of the National Socialist movement. Its rowdyism ran counter to his conservative, essentially bourgeois character, its violence to his strong attachment to law and justice."

DELUSIONS

Having resigned as Mayor of Leipzig, Goerdeler went to work for the Stuttgart industrialist Robert Bosch, and it was in his capacity as Bosch's financial adviser that he was able to establish contacts in Germany and abroad with groups opposed to Hitler. Supported by Robert Bosch and his opposi-tional Stuttgart Circle, Goerdeler spent the next three years in journeys to Western Europe, North America and the Near East. He wrote copious reports on these trips and was prepared to share his views with individuals from all shades of the political spectrum. Remarkably he even sent his reports to Hermann Göring and to Hitler's adjutant, which suggests that he had not entirely given up exercising a moderating influence on Nazi policy. Equally, such acts can be construed as political naïveté, even willful arrogance.

His friend Dr Hjalmar Schacht (President of the *Reichsbank*) called him a motor that ran too noisily! He was insensitive to political pressure and remained firmly convinced of the benevolence of human nature. As a result, he lacked political judgement and trusted people too easily. A number of the conspirators

The army on parade in Berlin on the occasion of Hitler's 50th birthday, 20 April 1939. On the eve of World War II the rejuvenated army held the Führer in high esteem – but there were still committed anti-Hitler senior officers.

against Hitler (particularly Stauffenberg) found Goerdeler too talkative and too indiscreet to be fully trusted. His message, however, was simple: the international community desired peace – particularly Britain – Germany was under no military threat from the outside world, and could therefore achieve a peaceful revision of its frontiers provided it did not ask for too much, too soon. In time it became clear to Goerdeler

General von Fritsch, Army Commander-in-Chief 1934–38. At first pro-Hitler, he had confined the army to barracks during the Röhm purge. He later opposed the invasions of Austria and Czechoslovakia, and was forced to resign his post.

Field Marshal Erwin von Witzleben fought in Poland and France in 1939–40, but was retired from active service in 1942 for not being totally committed to the Nazi cause. Involved in the Bomb Plot, he was hanged after its failure.

that Hitler would have to be overthrown if Germany was to be spared the catastrophe of total defeat, and that a *coup d'état* could only be successfully undertaken with the help of the armed forces. During the next few years, he repeatedly attempted to persuade high-ranking military leaders to overthrow Hitler.

Having renewed old relations with Ludwig Beck at the end of 1936, by the summer of 1938 the two were building up the core of an élite national-conservative opposition to Hitler. Beck and Goerdeler formed an unlikely combination; Beck was reticent whereas Goerdeler was a tireless intriguer and networker. Nevertheless, through their contacts with the learned Berlin Wednesday Club (see Chapter 4) they succeeded in bringing together a coalition of like-minded conservatives opposed to Hitler's expansionist foreign policy.

A significant figure in this growing circle was Lieutenant-Colonel (later Brigadier-General) Hans Oster, director of the central department of the *Abwehr* and a resolute opponent of Hitler. Oster's antipathy to the

> ## *Oster's antipathy to the regime was fostered by the Nazi treatment of von Fritsch*

regime was fostered by the Nazi treatment of Fritsch, who had during their period of common service become a personal friend. In the course of the crisis Rear Admiral (later Admiral) Wilhelm Canaris, chief of the *Abwehr*, had introduced him to Beck for the first time. Oster was a selfless man of ideals who could inspire tremendous enthusiasm. Hans-Bernd Gisevius (an important Gestapo informant for Oster and the *Abwehr*) in his book, *To the Last Bitter End*, quotes Oster as saying to him: "To our last breath we must remain upstanding men, as we were taught to be from childhood and by our soldierly discipline ... We fear the wrath of God will fall upon us only if we are not straight and decent and fail to do our duty."

Both Canaris and Oster viewed the expansion of the SS and its lack of principles and discipline, and the eclipse of the army, as matters of national concern. The *Abwehr* provided both men with an excellent operational base. The German Security and Intelligence Services could be traced back to

Frederick the Great, but had been wound up in 1919 by the Treaty of Versailles. In 1920, a unit was set up to protect the armed forces from enemy (*bolshevik*) spies and radical agitators. It became part of the army's

Field Marshal von Blomberg, Minister of Defence 1933–38, saw Hitler as a strong man. However, he opposed the reoccupation of the Rhineland and the planned takeover of Czechoslovakia. Hitler forced him to resign following a sex scandal.

Field Marshal von Blomberg is congratulated by Hitler for 40 years of service in the army. Blomberg had a large responsibility for delivering the army into Hitler's hands, having taken an oath of loyalty to him in person.

"Statistical Department" – a cover name for Military Intelligence. In 1928, Naval Intelligence was incorporated and in 1932 Captain Conrad Patzig became head of the entire unit. In 1934, control passed to Heinrich Himmler, who extended the Prussian Secret State Police (*Geheime Staatspolizei* or Gestapo) to cover the entire Reich and amalgamated it with the Security Service (*Sicherheitsdienst* or SD), which since 1931 had been one of the three main components of the SS and was particularly concerned with collecting intelligence about domestic conditions. When Himmler made the ambitious and unscrupulous Reinhard Heydrich Chief of the Security Police, one of his main objectives was to take over responsibility for military and foreign intelligence from the armed forces. Patzig was removed for attempting to resist these changes and replaced by Canaris, who became director of the *Abwehr* in 1935 and was destined to play a considerable part in the opposition to Adolf Hitler.

Of the office's three main departments, *Abwehr I* collected information, *Abwehr II* organized sabotage abroad and *Abwehr III* dealt with counterintelligence. While the *Abwehr* was a bastion of orthodox conservatism, it would be wrong to give the impression that it was a hotbed of subversion. In a staff of some 13,000, it has been estimated that around 50 officers were committed anti-Nazis.

While Canaris was content to play a secondary role in opposition circles, and in fact never did break completely from the regime, Oster, on the other hand, was more

Hitler reviews SS troops in Hamburg. The army totally underestimated the potential threat of Himmler's SS organization, particularly the Gestapo, which infiltrated and broke up the various resistance groups.

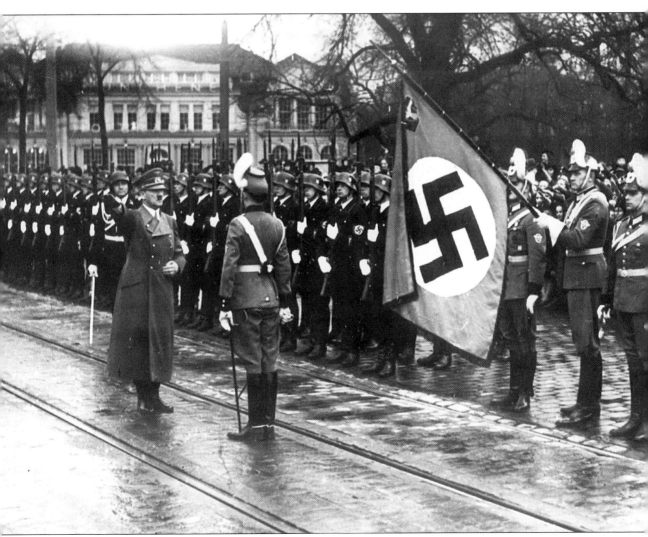

impulsive and imaginative. It was Canaris who was the first to tell Beck of the plot to oust Fritsch. His efforts to rehabilitate the disgraced former Commander-in-Chief and, in turn, discredit the Gestapo drew him closer to Oster. Ernst von Weizscker, another officer in the *Abwehr*, said of Canaris that he was "one of the most interesting phenomena of the period, a type brought to light and perfected under dictatorship, a combination of disinterested idealism and shrewdness that is particularly rare in Germany. There one rarely finds the cleverness of a snake and the purity of a dove combined in one character." The two counterintelligence officers went on to form a mutually dependent team and an important conduit for various resistance groups.

> ## There can be no doubt that Oster was the dominant and more influential partner

Both men recognized that they could only work effectively against Hitler if they managed to retain their positions of authority, which often meant carrying out Hitler's orders. There can, however, be no doubt that Oster was the dominant and more influential partner. While Canaris often provided cover for Oster's subversive activities by means of his undoubted skills in intrigue and subterfuge, it was Oster who built up a cadre of loyal followers within the *Abwehr*, and in other sections of the *Reichswehr*. These invariably turned out to be men of similar nature to Oster: contemptuous of "parlour" opposition and sworn to action. More will be said of this later.

THE FIRST COUP PLANS

In August 1938, Beck drafted the first plan for a *coup d'état* in the event of an invasion of Czechoslovakia. General Halder, Beck's successor, had agreed to take the initiative against Hitler as he was officially responsible for preparing the invasion. This order might be given as little as 24 hours before troops were to cross the border. If, as expected, Hitler did not abandon his policy, then the

British Prime Minister Neville Chamberlain following his return from the Munich Conference in September 1938. The British and French acquiescence to Hitler's demands ruined a potential military coup led by Beck and Halder.

Höpner (on left) as a panzer group commander during Operation Barbarossa, the German invasion of the Soviet Union in June 1941. Höpner was dismissed by Hitler in January 1942 for disobeying orders to hold his position.

group around Beck intended to overthrow the government between the time that Hitler gave the order to attack and the actual beginning of hostilities. Within that time Halder was expected to give the signal for the coup. On Beck's advice, Halder asked Oster what preparations, both political and technical, had been made for the coup. Hans-

Bernd Gisevius, a friend of Oster's who was then working in the office of the Gestapo, was deeply involved in the coup, and so was Hans von Dohnanyi. Moreover, General von Witzleben, General von Brockdorff, General Höpner, the Berlin Chief of Police Count von Helldorf and his Deputy, Fritz-Dietlof von der Schulenburg, had also agreed to take part. Indeed, III Army Corps had promised to act, if necessary, without Halder's agreement.

Units were designated to occupy key points and government buildings. There was some dispute in the conspiracy as to whether Hitler should be put on trial or summarily executed – in fact this contradiction was never fully resolved. Beck and Halder did not contemplate assassination, whereas members of the *Abwehr*'s shock troops, whose leader was First Lieutenant Heinz, intended to shoot Hitler upon his arrest.

BRITISH SUPPORT?

The coup was to be given foreign support by asking Britain, as Czechoslovakia's guarantor power, to assume an unyielding stance towards Hitler, since his overthrow would be made easier after a serious foreign policy setback. Oster sent his confidant, Ewald von Kleist, to speak with Winston Churchill, while the permanent Under Secretary of State, Ernst Baron von Weizsäcker, had briefed Lord Halifax, the British Foreign Secretary, through an emissary (Theo Kordt) in the German Foreign Embassy in London.

General Erich Höpner stands in the People's Court following the failed attempt on Hitler's life in July 1944. Looking gaunt and tired, he was sentenced to death by Freisler on the charge of high treason and died by strangulation.

However, the British remained distrustful of all German opposition. Moreover, Prime Minister Chamberlain believed that the country was not ready for war. A general mobilization order was expected in Germany during the early afternoon of 28 September 1938, whereupon the conspirators planned to strike. But in the afternoon news came of an international conference to be held in Munich. The following day Chamberlain, French Premier Daladier, Hitler and Mussolini agreed that the Sudetenland should be transferred to Germany, while guaranteeing the remaining Czech frontiers. On 30 September, Hitler and Chamberlain signed the infamous "peace in our time" communiqué. The planned *coup d'état* against the Führer was now impossible.

THE BÜRGERBRÄUKELLER

After the failure of the 1938 Putsch, the next serious threat on Hitler's life came from an individual with no connections to the military, or indeed to any other resistance group. This was the so-called Bürgerbräu assassination attempt. In commemoration of Hitler's failed Putsch of November 1923, the "Old Fighters" had gathered in Munich ever since 1933 for a memorial day for those Nazi "martyrs" killed in 1923. The event consisted of a re-enactment of the march to the Feldherrnhalle and a ceremony outside the Temple of Honour on the Königsplatz.

The main attraction, however, was a speech by Hitler to a gathering of the Party faithful on the evening of 8 November in the Bürgerbräukeller. The previous year a Swiss Catholic theology student, Maurice Bavaud, attempted to assassinate Hitler at the same event. Having stalked Hitler for weeks, Bavaud intended to shoot the Führer as he headed the annual march along the streets of Munich. Pretending to be a journalist for a Swiss newspaper, he managed to obtain a front row seat on the reviewing stand and carried a loaded pistol. However, as Hitler approached, SA troops stood up to give the Nazi salute and obscured his view. Bavaud had to abandon the assassination attempt, but he hoped to try again later. However, after following Hitler to Berchtesgaden, he

> ## Bavaud intended to shoot Hitler as he headed the annual Munich march

ran out of funds and boarded the train for the French border. He was arrested in Augsburg, having been discovered without a valid ticket. The gun was found on him, and he confessed his intentions under Gestapo interrogation. He was tried by the People's Court in December 1939, sentenced to death and beheaded in 1941, after Swiss efforts to save his life finally collapsed.

A year after Bavaud's unsuccessful assassination attempt, a disaffected south German cabinet maker, Georg Elser, attempted to kill Hitler at the same event. Elser was born in January 1903 in Hermaringen in the district of Heidenheim. He was a trained cabinet maker, worked for various firms in Upper Swabia, and became unemployed during the economic crisis of 1930. He was a non-practising Protestant and was not ideologically or politically committed. However, he had decisively rejected National Socialism claiming, under interrogation, that he was convinced that a war was inevitable. Elser visited Munich in 1938 for the Nazi Party gathering and had used the opportunity to familiarize himself with the site. It is strange to think that the two assassins' paths almost certainly crossed in the streets of Munich.

Elser returned to Munich at the beginning of August 1939 and set about his preparations, living off his savings. In the day he worked on his clock and the bomb in his lodgings, and at night he visited the Bürgerbräukeller where he made meticulous plans for hiding a bomb in a pillar close to where Hitler would deliver his speech. Hiding in the hall after it was closed, he spent approximately 30 to 35 nights hollowing out the column. On the evening of 1 November he began to install it, found various adjustments necessary, but had

Freikorps members outside the Bürgerbräukeller in Munich, just prior to the 1923 Beer Hall Putsch. It was later the scene of two failed assassination attempts against Hitler, in November 1938 and November 1939.

completed it by the night of 5–6 November. He then took his belongings to his sister in Stuttgart, intending to continue across the Swiss border. But on the night of 7–8 November he returned again to make sure that the clock on the machine was working.

A Red Army T-34 tank races past the body of a German soldier in Russia in early 1942. While the army was winning there were few dissenting military voices against Hitler, but things began to change after the reverses of 1942–43 in the East.

On 8 November he travelled to Konstanz and set out to cross the Swiss frontier.

Hitler usually began his speech at 20:30 hours and then spoke until 22:00 hours. On 8 November 1939, the Führer began his speech 30 minutes earlier than usual

and ended it at 21:07 hours. Then, instead of staying on to chat with old comrades, he left to catch his special train back to Berlin. The bomb went off at 21:20 hours, killing eight and wounding 63. It would almost certainly have killed Hitler had he still been standing at the rostrum. While Hitler was speaking in the Bürgerbräukeller, Elser was arrested by two German custom officials while attempting to cross the Swiss border illegally. Notes concerning the production of munitions, a postcard of the Bürgerbräukeller, a pair of pliers, several suspicious pieces of metal, and other things were found on his person.

THE HIGHEST BRAVERY

This miscellaneous collection aroused suspicion when news of the explosion came through. Elser was transferred to Munich and then Berlin where, under severe Gestapo interrogation, he gave a detailed account of his activities.

Opponents of the regime at home and abroad were convinced that the assassination attempt had been a put-up job to boost Hitler's popularity. Himmler, on the other hand, had persuaded Hitler that Elser must have been working with the British secret service. Elser was interrogated in the Reich Main Security Office in Berlin for weeks, but even under severe torture he provided no names. Eventually he was sent to Sachsenhausen but given favourable treatment as a special prisoner of Hitler. He is thought to have been kept alive for use as a key witness against the British secret service in a show trial after the war. Elser was transferred to Dachau at the end of 1944 or early 1945. When the imminent collapse of Nazism could no longer be resisted, Elser – the man who nearly liberated Germany from Hitler – was murdered on 9 April 1945, on orders from the "highest authority".

In the wake of these assassination attempts security measures were tightened considerably. The commemorative march was never held again, and Hitler's increasingly rare public appearances were protected by vast security operations.

In the late 1930s and early 1940s, the doubts of a number of military commanders were temporarily stilled by the successes at Munich, in Poland, in Scandinavia and in France. From May 1940 until defeat at Stalingrad in late 1942, Hitler's standing in

the eyes of the public was so great that all thoughts of removing him from office were impossible, and would have been counterproductive. By 1941, public confidence was so high, and belief in the Führer's protean powers so great, that few generals sought to stop him from attacking Russia and thus committing Germany to a war on two fronts. The conspirators therefore had to bide their time and hope for military reversals. These occurred in the severe winter of 1941–42, when German armies suffered their first setbacks in the Russian campaign. Changes had also taken place within the military leadership; von Brauchitsch resigned, von Witzleben was retired and Höpner was downgraded. These changes in turn created uncertainties – and opportunities.

Meanwhile, throughout these discouraging setbacks Carl Goerdeler remained the most indefatigable opponent of Hitler. He continued to travel abroad extensively, warning governments of Hitler's intentions.

> *The conspirators had to bide their time and hope for military reversals*

After the occupation of Prague in March 1939, he wrote to highly placed officials in London, Paris and Washington, urging world leaders to impose sanctions on Germany and to issue a call to the German people to rise up and overthrow Nazism. He also continued to impress upon civilian and military resistance circles the necessity of acting against Hitler.

Late in 1941, Goerdeler completed his ideas for constitutional and social reorganization in the memorandum *Das Ziel* (*The Goal*) written in close collaboration with Beck. Goerdeler had also redoubled his efforts to win the cooperation of influential army officers in overthrowing Hitler. Those he impressed included von Falkenhausen and von Stülpnagel, the commanders in Belgium and France, and General Field Marshal von Kluge, Supreme Commander of the Central Army Group on the Eastern Front. Goerdeler made a particular impact on Major-General Henning von Tresckow, von Kluge's First General Staff Officer. Goerdeler called him "the best opposition soldier" and von Tresckow saw in Goerdeler the future Chancellor of Germany.

VON TRESCKOW

Major-General Henning von Tresckow was born in Magdeburg in 1901. The von Tresckows had served in the Prussian and German armies for 300 years. Von Tresckow had served with distinction as a young officer in World War I and had stayed on in the *Reichswehr* for two years afterwards, when he left the army and took a job on the Berlin stock exchange. As a captain on the General Staff, von Tresckow had protested to General von Witzleben at the failure of the army to counter the trumped-up charges against Fritsch.

He also rejected Hitler's policy of aggression. In December 1940 he took up the post of Head of the Operations Section of the Central Army Group in the forthcoming Russian campaign under his uncle, Field Marshal von Bock. Through his cousin, Fabian von Schlabrendorff, whom he had assigned to his unit as an ordnance officer, he maintained contact with Goerdeler and Oster and the conspirators in Berlin. Von Tresckow discovered on the staff of the Central Army Group a number of officers who remained sceptical about the campaign in the East, and who

were appalled at the treatment of Russian prisoners as laid down by Hitler, as well as the high casualties the army was suffering. These sceptics included Count Heinrich von Lendorff, a wealthy landowner in East Prussia and adjutant to Bock, and Major-General Baron Rudolf von Gersdorff. Von Tresckow had attempted to persuade Bock to get these orders withdrawn. But the field marshal would not confront Hitler

personally and Gersdorff, whom he sent instead, was unable to meet with the Führer. When the German invasion came to a halt outside Moscow, von Tresckow informed Bock that the army would suffer an historic defeat from which it would never recover, and that Hitler would have to be removed. Although Bock was not part of the conspiracy, he was removed on Hitler's orders and replaced by von Kluge, who came

Germans troops near Lake Il'men on the Eastern Front. Officers such as Major-General von Tresckow soon became disillusioned with the war against the Soviet Union and began to establish links with anti-Nazi conspirators.

increasingly to share von Tresckow's views regarding the Supreme Commander.

Throughout 1942, von Tresckow continued to press von Kluge of the imperative need to act. In the meantime, links between the front and the conspirators in Berlin were drawn closer. In April, Gersdorff acquired supplies of captured British explosives and fuses via the *Abwehr*. In November, a secret visit to the front was arranged for Goerdeler, who greatly impressed von Kluge. At a meeting in Berlin in December, Goerdeler and General Friedrich Olbricht, head of the General War Office in the Replacement Army, agreed to have contingency plans for Operation Flash ready in six weeks, after which von

> *Beck and Goerdeler were ready to take their appointed places in the temporary regime*

Tresckow would persuade von Kluge to raise the standard of revolt at the front.

Beck and Goerdeler were ready to take their appointed places in the temporary regime that would be set up: Beck as coordinator of the military and police and Goerdeler as head of the civil administration. The spring of 1943 was regarded as the ideal time to implement the coup. The German people had been badly shaken by the capitulation of Field Marshal Paulus' Sixth Army at Stalingrad, and the final rout

SCHELLENBERG

Walter Schellenberg, a senior SS counter-intelligence officer who broke up many anti-Hitler groups in 1944 and 1945. Ironically, he also established contacts with the Red Cross and US intelligence, no doubt to save his own skin.

of Field Marshal Erwin Rommel's army in North Africa. In March, a visit by Admiral Canaris and other *Abwehr* officers to von Kluge's army headquarters enabled von Tresckow and Oster's assistant, von Dohnanyi, to agree on mutual notification and support. A few days later, on 13 March, an opportunity presented itself when Hitler agreed to a request to visit von Kluge in Smolensk. Von Kluge, however, explicitly forbade an open pistol attack. During lunch von Tresckow asked Colonel Brandt, who travelled on Hitler's personal aeroplane, to deliver a couple of bottles of Cointreau back to friends at headquarters in Berlin. Brandt agreed and Schlabrendorff handed him a small parcel containing two British "clam" explosives, along with a silent pencil-shaped time-fuse set to explode in 30 minutes.

Hitler's plane did not crash because the bombs failed to explode. Schlabrendorff flew to Hitler's headquarters on the next courier flight to retrieve the parcel, claiming an error. On examining the bomb-parcel he discovered that the fuse had functioned but the detonator-cap had failed to ignite the explosive.

MORE DISAPPOINTMENTS

In spite of this disappointment, von Tresckow made another attempt to have Hitler killed just a few days later, this time by Rudolf von Gersdorff. The occasion selected was the opening of an exhibition of captured war material in Berlin on 21 March. The opening by Hitler was part of the annual commemorative ceremony for the dead of World War I. Gersdorff had come to Berlin to conduct Hitler around the exhibition, and had agreed with von Tresckow that he would conceal in his pockets the two bombs that had failed to detonate in the aeroplane attempt. He had received them from Schlabrendorff, with 10-minute delay fuses, on 20 March, the day he arrived in Berlin.

But this plan also failed because Hitler went through the exhibition too quickly, and Gersdorff retired hastily to a lavatory and detached the fuses. His conspiracy was never discovered and he survived the war. Von Tresckow and his co-conspirators listened to the uneventful ceremony from the Russian Front with bitter disappointment.

CANARIS IS DISMISSED

The Gestapo, meanwhile, was becoming increasing nervous after Stalingrad and the "White Rose" demonstrations organized by the Scholls. The *Abwehr* ceased to be an important central link for German resistance when, in April 1943, von Dohnanyi, Müller and Bonhöffer were arrested in conjunction with an investigation into foreign currency irregularities, and Hans Oster was removed from office. Despite prolonging legal proceedings against *Abwehr* collaborators, its chief, Admiral Canaris, was eventually dismissed in February 1944 and later placed under house arrest, while the remaining section of the *Abwehr* was directly subordinated to the Security Service of the SS.

The opponents of Hitler experienced a series of misfortunes in 1943 and 1944. Some of these can be put down to bad luck, but mention must also be made of the growing efficiency of the Nazi security forces under Himmler and Walter Schellenberg.

The elimination of Oster's office was a major setback for the resistance. Von Tresckow made one final attempt on Hitler's life in November 1943, proposing that the Führer should be blown up while inspecting

new uniforms modelled by upstanding young officers in Rastenburg. In November 1943 and February 1944, two officers, Axel von der Bussche and Ewald-Heinrich von Kleist-Shmenzin, volunteered to sacrifice themselves in the same way as Gersdorff. However, the new military equipment was destroyed in an air raid and the inspection was postponed. And in February the demonstration was again cancelled. In March Captain von Breitenbuch agreed to kill

> *The co-conspirators listened to the uneventful ceremony with bitter disappointment*

Hitler with a pistol shot when he went to an interview with the Führer in attendance with von Kluge's successor, only to be stopped by an SS man from entering the room.

Von Tresckow, Schlabrendorff and their comrades never again got within killing range of Hitler. In many respects it is questionable whether the Bussche and Kleist plans belong to the "von Tresckow phase" of conspiracies to kill Hitler, or whether they should be regarded as a part of the prelude to the July 1944 Bomb Plot, which is widely considered to represent the dramatic final conspiracy organized by military resistance.

Upon his return to Berlin in July 1943, von Tresckow began to rework the Operation Valkyrie plans for the suppression of internal uprisings to serve as the basis of an anti-Hitler *coup d'état*. His closest collaborator in this was the severely wounded Colonel Claus Schenk von Stauffenberg, who finally carried out the assassination attempt.

Count Schenk von Stauffenberg, born in 1907, was the son of a Swabian-Frankish noble family whose father was an official at the court of the King of Württemberg. In 1926 Stauffenberg joined the 17th Bamberg Cavalry Regiment (the so-called *Bamberger Reiter*). From 1936 to 1938 he attended the War Academy in Berlin where he was referred to as the "new Schlieffen". In 1938 he joined the élite of the reformed General Staff. He took part in the Polish and French campaigns, and in April 1943 was severely wounded in Tunis, losing his left eye, his

> ## Stauffenberg believed that the officer corps should assume responsibility for the nation

right arm and two fingers on his left hand. After spending months in military hospitals, he became Chief of Staff in the General Army Office under General Olbricht, with the rank of colonel.

When the Nazis came to power he was one of those officers who initially accepted them as a lesser evil than the failing Weimar regime. He welcomed the *Anschluss* with Austria and was impressed with the early victories over Poland and France. However, he soon realized that a "final victory" would have as many dire consequences for Germany as the defeat which he concluded was inevitable.

In the summer of 1942, having learned of the mass murder of Jews and other civilians, as well as millions of prisoners-of-war in the occupied Soviet Union, he became convinced that by eliminating Hitler the war could be ended and the senseless deaths of millions of people prevented. Stauffenberg had decided not only to assume responsibility for organizing the coup, he also decided to carry out the assassination himself. (He believed that the officer corps alone should assume

responsibility for the fate of the nation.) While recovering from his wounds, he spent August and September in Berlin meeting key figures such as Beck, Goerdeler and Leber, and in working with von Tresckow on plans to implement Operation Valkyrie, allowing the military to protect key points in Berlin and the main provincial cities.

Everything hinged on Hitler being eliminated. On 1 July 1944, Stauffenberg was appointed Chief of Staff of the Replacement Army under General Fromm. This gave him access to the situation briefings in the Führer's headquarters. On 11 July Stauffenberg flew, with a bomb in his briefcase, to Obersalzburg. He decided not to set it off, since Himmler was not present.

At the next meeting on 15 July at the Rastenburg headquarters, Stauffenberg's freedom of action was limited by Fromm's presence and by the fact that Hitler ended the briefing ahead of schedule. Acting under instructions from Stauffenberg, in Berlin Olbricht had set in motion the first stages of Operation Valkyrie. On hearing that Hitler had left the meeting early, Olbricht had to hastily countermand earlier instructions under the pretext that it had been a drill. Earlier, on 4 July, the prominent social democratic opponent of Hitler, Adolf Reichwein, was arrested while attending a communist underground meeting, and the following day the Gestapo arrested Julius Leber, one of the inner circle of conspirators and a friend of Stauffenberg.

The conspirators now had to work under the constant fear that Leber would break under Gestapo torture and reveal names. Moreover, some of the conspirators, notably Stauffenberg, came to fear that Goerdeler was becoming a security risk. Accordingly, details of the military plans were withheld from him. On 17 July, news that Goerdeler was being seen as the future Chancellor reached the

Graf Claus Schenk von Stauffenberg, the officer who planted the bomb that exploded at Rastenburg on 20 July 1944. When the attempt failed he was shot on the evening of the 20th. His last words were: "Long live sacred Germany."

Gestapo, who immediately issued a warrant for his arrest. On 19 July Goerdeler was secretly taken out of Berlin for his own safety and, as a result, played no part in the dramatic events that followed.

These reverses merely strengthened Stauffenberg's resolve. On 18 July he learnt that he would attend another conference at Rastenburg on 20 July. At 06:00 hours on that day Stauffenberg drove out to Rangsdorf airfield, south of Berlin. He had wrapped the bomb in a shirt and placed it in his briefcase. It was the same type of delayed-fuse bomb that had been used by von Tresckow and Schlabrendorff, and it was timed to go off within 10 minutes of the detonating process being set in motion.

Because Stauffenberg was indispensable to the success of Operation Valkyrie, the plan was for him to leave the briefing room before the explosion. On arriving at the *Wolfschanze* (Wolf's Lair) in Rastenburg, Stauffenberg made contact with General Erich Fellgiebel, Chief of Signal Troops, who was to telephone news of Hitler's death to the conspirators in Berlin. Upon hearing the news, General Olbricht and his new Chief of Staff, Colonel Albrecht Mertz von Quirnheim, would immediately set in train a series of moves under the codename Valkyrie, to seize executive control.

THE BOMB EXPLODES

The briefing was brought forward from 13:00 hours to 12:30 hours, because Mussolini was due to arrive in the afternoon for a private meeting with Hitler. As the headquarters was being reconstructed, the meeting took place in a barrack room with a cavity below the wooden floor. Because it was a very hot day all 10 windows in the room were open. So as not to attract the suspicion of Field Marshal Keitel (who was chairing the preliminary session), Stauffenberg had mentioned to an officer in earshot of Keitel on his way to the meeting that he was expecting a telephone call from Berlin with information for the Führer. Together with his staff officer, First Lieutenant Werner von Haeften, Stauffenberg

Hitler shows Mussolini the shattered conference room where Stauffenberg placed the bomb. The latter could not place the bomb right next to Hitler, and the force of the explosion was dissipated by the windows and lightweight roof.

had set the timer of the bomb during an interval between several preliminary briefings. However, since they had been disturbed while doing this, Stauffenberg was able to set only half of the explosives that he had intended to detonate. When he entered the conference chamber he placed the explosive device, which was hidden in his briefcase, against an oak support of the large map table near Hitler, who had already begun the discussion of the military situation. There were now 24 persons in the room. After a minute or so, Stauffenberg left the room to make the bogus telephone call.

The bomb detonated at approximately 12:45 hours with a deafening thud. The official stenographer, Heinrich Berger, was killed and three officers, including Colonel Heinz Brandt (who had unsuspectingly carried von Tresckow's two bombs with him in March 1943 on the flight from Smolensk to Rastenburg), died subsequently from their injuries. Hitler survived. His eardrums were perforated, his hair singed, his right leg had been burned and his right arm badly bruised. "I am invulnerable, I am immortal!", the

An injured Hitler following the July Bomb Plot. Revenge was swift and merciless, both against the conspirators and their families. Those sentenced to death were killed by firing squad, the guillotine or slow strangulation.

Führer kept repeating to Dr Morell as he treated his injuries. After washing and changing he received Mussolini and showed the astonished Italian dictator the ruins of the briefing room.

Having seen and heard the explosion, Stauffenberg and Haeften assumed that Hitler was dead and left for the airport in a pre-arranged car. They did not arrive in Berlin until four hours later. General

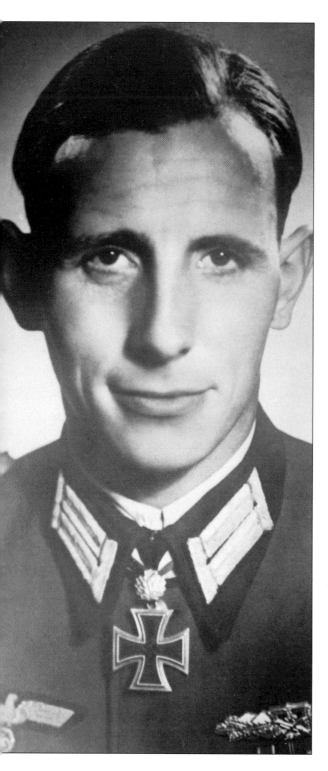

Otto Ernst Remer, the commander of the Guard Battalion in Berlin during the July Bomb Plot. Having talked with Hitler on the telephone after the assassination attempt, he was ordered to crush the rising – which he did ruthlessly.

Fellgiebel had meanwhile telephoned the conspirators in Berlin, who were waiting to implement Operation Valkyrie. Fellgiebel's call was received by General Fritz Thiele, head of the Signals Branch of Army Headquarters. In guarded language (presumably so as not to compromise Stauffenberg), Fellgiebel confirmed that the assassination attempt had been made, but indicated that Hitler was still alive. The coordinators in Berlin, namely Olbricht and Thiele, did not know what to make of the news and prevaricated.

At 15:00 hours Stauffenberg and Haeften landed in Berlin, and Haeften then telephoned them to confirm that Hitler was dead. Olbricht asked Fromm to issue the Valkyrie orders. Fromm refused. Olbricht and Mertz von Quirnheim (Stauffenberg's successor as Chief of Staff to Olbricht) then issued the orders themselves at approximately 16:00 hours. This proved a lengthy business, as separate orders had to be teleprinted to each destination. By the time Stauffenberg and Haeften arrived at reserve Army High Command headquarters at the Bendlerstrasse at 16:30 hours, Fromm had heard from Keitel at the *Wolfschanze* that Hitler had only been slightly injured in the bomb blast. Stauffenberg now took command of the situation and ordered Fromm's arrest.

General Beck, plus General Höpner, Chief of Police Count von Helldorf and other conspirators, now arrived at the Bendlerstrasse to be briefed. Höpner, who had been dismissed in disgrace by Hitler in January 1942, took over Fromm's post. Beck telephoned von

Kluge at La Roche Guyon, German Army headquarters in France, to confirm his support. Von Kluge, as usual, would not commit himself but promised to ring back in 30 minutes. He never did. Beck is reported to have said: "There's Kluge for you." Although Stauffenberg repeatedly confirmed to as many military circles as possible that Hitler was dead and that General Beck and Field Marshal von Witzleben had assumed control, he failed to silence growing doubts.

> ## Stauffenberg, Olbricht and the others were taken down to the courtyard and shot

When Lieutenant-General von Hase, the Berlin Chief of Police and a conspirator, ordered Major Remer, the commander of the Berlin Guard Battalion stationed at Moabit, to cordon off the government quarter, one of Goebbels' Army Propaganda officers, Lieutenant Hagen, happened to be in Remer's office. Hagen thought Hase's orders suspicious and insisted on reporting the situation to Goebbels, who until that time was unaware of the coup. The Propaganda Minister had Remer brought to him and put him through to the Führer's headquarters on a private line. Hitler promoted Remer to colonel on the spot and authorized him to crush the coup with all available means.

By now Stauffenberg's plans were beginning to turn sour. At 18:30 hours national radio (which the conspirators had failed to seize) broadcast the failure of the attempted assassination and Hitler's survival. Stauffenberg could no longer insist to the regional army commander that his orders be followed. Around 20:00 hours,

Field Marshal von Witzleben arrived at the Bendlerstrasse, but left within the hour, convinced that the coup had failed. At 22:00 hours, a group of officers loyal to Hitler freed General Fromm after some shooting and held Stauffenberg, Beck, Olbricht, Mertz and Haeften.

Fromm conducted an immediate court-martial, no doubt to prevent incriminating evidence being given to the Gestapo, and ordered them to be shot. Beck was allowed to commit suicide – but he only wounded himself and was finished off by a sergeant in the Guard Battalion. Stauffenberg, Olbricht and the others were taken down to the courtyard and shot by a firing squad. As Stauffenberg fell he shouted: "Long live sacred Germany." Shortly before his arrest Stauffenberg had spoken with Colonel von Listow in Paris, informing him that in Berlin everything was lost. What he didn't know was that in Paris, Brussels, Prague and Vienna the operation had gone according to plan. Troops were set in motion and Nazi officials arrested; in Paris the entire SS and SD establishment had been disarmed and their headquarters occupied.

CONCLUSIONS

In retrospect it is easy to see that crucial mistakes were made. In assuming the joint role of *coup d'état* leader and assassin, Stauffenberg was forced to act in two places, more than 480km (300 miles) apart. This proved a daunting and onerous responsibility for a single person to undertake – made all the more difficult by Stauffenberg's severe physical disabilities. We should never forget, however, that he almost succeeded. The irony of 20 July 1944 was that it ultimately failed not because Hitler survived, but due to the vacillations and indecisiveness of those generals who failed to implement the Valkyrie orders. In his account of the failed assassination plot written after the war, Schlabrendorff claimed: "We were not natural revolutionaries; for our strength lay in the officers and officials who took part. Blood should have run – instead the men of 20 July said to all and sundry: 'Have a seat.'"

Most of the remaining conspirators in the Home Army Command were arrested around midnight. In the early hours of the morning of 21 July, Hitler broadcast to the nation and announced the failure of the plot by "a very small clique of ambitious officers, devoid of conscience and criminally stupid." In one

> ## "A small clique of ambitious officers, devoid of conscience and criminally stupid"

sense Hitler was right: there were 2000 generals in the *Wehrmacht* in 1944; only 22 lost their lives as a result of the failed conspiracy of 20 July. However, hundreds of arrests followed as the Gestapo set about destroying the last vestiges of the German resistance movement. A number of those who were involved in the planning and operational stages of the coup committed suicide.

Henning von Tresckow was not directly involved, but he knew that his name would be connected with the resistance. He committed suicide on 21 July rather than be tortured into revealing the names of his co-conspirators. His great friend Fabian von Schlabrendorff (who had buried von Tresckow's body in the family grave) was arrested and brutally tortured on 17 August, and then taken to Sachsenhausen camp and later made to watch while von Tresckow's coffin was opened and the corpse incinerated. Schlabrendorff was finally put before Roland Freisler and the People's Court

on 3 February 1945, when an Allied bombing raid destroyed the court, including Freisler, and the incriminating documents.

Schlabrendorff survived the war, and from 1967 to 1975 was a Judge of the Federal Constitutional Court. Von Kluge, who had been unable to make up his mind during the coup, took his life by poisoning himself when ordered to report to Berlin. Carl Goerdeler, who had been in hiding, returned to Berlin on 25 July and stayed in a number of safe houses until 8 August, when he decided that escape was no longer

Field Marshal von Kluge, who refused to join the Bomb Plot conspirators but promised help if Hitler was killed. He was relieved of all duties in August 1944 and ordered back to Germany from France. He committed suicide by taking poison.

February 1945. His last months in prison proved particularly lonely and depressing as he cut an isolated figure, increasingly removed from reality.

On 7 February 1945, Canaris, Oster and Halder were moved from Berlin to Flossenbürg camp. They had successfully manage to conceal the extent of their activities, although the Gestapo remained convinced that they were involved in the plot to kill Hitler. The massing of troops to defend Berlin had led to the discovery of Canaris' diaries lodged by Oster and von Dohnanyi in safe keeping in the OKW Headquarters at Zossen. These records of Hitler's activities proved their undoing.

On hearing of their discovery and the possibility that they may have been used against him, an incandescent Hitler gave orders for the conspirators at Flossenbürg to be eliminated. Oster refused to support Canaris' story of only having gone along with the conspiracy in order to give it away at the last moment. Both were executed on 9 April.

RETRIBUTION

Colonel-General Fritz Fromm, who had summarily executed Stauffenberg, was summoned to the Ministry of Propaganda by Goebbels and arrested on suspicion of being involved in the coup. He was sentenced to death for cowardice and executed on 12 March 1945. The other conspirators had to defend their actions before the hysterical Freisler and the farcical People's Court. The primary offenders were executed within two hours of sentencing. They were strangled to death on Hitler's orders. The sentences were carried out in a shed at Plötzensee prison in the northwestern part of Berlin. The condemned men were strangled slowly with thin wire suspended from meat hooks, and the executions were filmed in detail for Hitler to watch.

possible and fled to East Prussia. A reward of one million marks was offered to anyone identifying him. He was eventually arrested on 12 August, having been recognized by a former servant of his family. Although he was tried and condemned to death on 8 September, he was not executed until 2

LEGACIES

The fall of Nazi Germany did not end the conspiracies that surrounded National Socialism: the Allies shielded Nazi war criminals, others disappeared, while a myth of resistance began to take shape.

Comparatively early on in World War II, Germany's enemies declared that they intended to bring war criminals to justice. At the beginning of 1942, nine Allied nations declared that the punishment of war criminals by judicial process at the end of hostilities was one of their war aims. A War Crimes Commission was established to collect and collate the evidence and decide what to do about it. In November 1943 Great Britain, the United States and USSR declared that when the war was over war

The Red Army flies the flag of the Soviet Union over the shattered remains of Berlin in May 1945. In public the Allies were determined to bring Nazi criminals to justice, but both the US and USSR protected some Nazis for their own ends.

criminals would be handed over to the governments of the areas in which their crimes had been committed. In the case of major criminals whose crimes were not limited to specific areas, they would be tried by an international tribunal. The

Like many senior German officers, Minister of Defence Werner von Blomberg (left) believed Hitler would be a strong man who could restore order in Germany. But they all underestimated the Nazi leader's utter ruthlessness.

International War Crimes Tribunal was constituted in August 1945 by agreement between the British, American, Soviet and French governments, and subsequently conducted the Nuremberg Trials between 1946 and 1949. The trials among other things made a sweeping judgment on the SS. The International Military Tribunal found that the organization was guilty of the persecution and extermination of the Jews and the brutal running of the concentration camps, excesses during the administration of the occupied territories, the slave labour programme, and the mistreatment and murder of Allied prisoners-of-war. All members of the SS were deemed to be war criminals who had been involved in the planning and implementation of war crimes and undertaking crimes against humanity. Not all members of the SS, however, were prosecuted with the same vigour by the victorious Allies, and the latter took a very pragmatic approach when it came to Nazi individuals who could serve their own national interests.

Although the Allied powers had held the lead in many vital technological fields such as radar and, perhaps most importantly, atomic physics, there were a number of areas where German research and development far surpassed that of their opponents. Rocketry

was one such field, and from 1937 the technical director of the organization responsible for rocketry's development, the German Army Ordnance Office, was Wernher von Braun. Von Braun had joined the army's ballistic missile team in 1932, and while engaged in this work he received a PhD in aerospace engineering. The German Army rocket programme was moved from the Kummersdorf test range near Berlin to a small fishing village on the Baltic Sea called Peenemünde in the late 1930s. Von Braun's

A young boy steals potatoes during economic hardship in Germany in the early 1920s. Germans remembered such harrowing images, and were grateful to the Nazis for bringing economic prosperity to Germany in the 1930s.

team had the rough plans for a ballistic missile, the A-4, which could carry a ton of explosives over a range of 275km (172 miles) ready as early as 1936. The work continued apace through the war years, and the A-4 was successfully launched – at the third try – on 3 October 1942. In fact the rocket's capabilities had come on somewhat, and the 14m- (46ft-) long liquid oxygen- and alcohol-fuelled missile could deliver its 1000kg (2200lb) warhead up to a range of 800km (500 miles) at velocities in excess of 560km/h (350mph). It was ready for combat use by the autumn of 1944. On 8 September 1944 an A-4 rocket was successfully launched against London, hitting Chiswick and killing three people and injuring 17 more. Nazi Propaganda Minister Joseph Goebbels labelled the missile the *Vergeltungswaffen-2* (Reprisal Weapon-2) or V-2, and claimed that it was a weapon that could reverse the war. Some 1054 of these rockets were fired at Britain between 8 September 1944 and 27 March 1945, when Allied forces overran the last launch sites – 2700 Londoners died in these attacks. A further 900 V-2s were launched at the Dutch port of Antwerp.

V-2 PRODUCTION

Although von Braun declared to his staff: "Let's not forget that this is the beginning of a new era, the era of rocket-powered flight. It seems that this is another demonstration of the sad fact that so often new developments get nowhere until they are first applied as weapons." He remarked after the war that the V-2 "behaved perfectly, but on the wrong planet"; his staff had more down-to-earth attitudes. As one said: "Don't kid yourself – although von Braun may have had space dust in his eyes since childhood – most of us were pretty mad about the Allied bombing of Germany. When the first V-2 hit London, we had champagne. Why not? We were at war." What is not forgivable is their role in overseeing outright barbarity when it came to the production methods of the V-2 production line.

Full-scale production of the V-2 did not begin until May 1944. In an effort to avoid the depredations of Allied bombing, the Germans dispersed the production of the V-Weapons and, where possible, used factory facilities that were underground. The most important production centre for the V-2 was a massive complex built in former anhydrite and gypsum mines under Kaunstein in northern Thuringia, built between October 1943 and March 1944 under SS supervision

> **At least 4000 concentration camp inmates died at the rate of about 100 a day**

in appalling conditions by concentration camp inmates, of whom at least 4000 died at the rate of about 100 a day. Once the system was up and running, as many as 40,000 prisoners in the factory and separate camp complex *Mittelbrau-Dora* worked on the subterranean production lines, producing up to 600 rockets a month. The dead piled up at the end of each day "as remarked upon as worn brushes or broken tools". In the words of Michael Burleigh in his excellent *The Third Reich: A New History*: "All this occurred under the indifferent gaze of German engineers and foreman, notably the chief rocket scientist professor Wernher von Braun."

By the beginning of 1945 it was clear to von Braun that Germany would lose the war, and he began to prepare for the post-war world. He had his men hide much of the vital data concerning the German rocket programme in the Harz Mountains, and engineered the surrender of himself and some 500 scientists from his programme to the Americans. The American military – some 10 years behind the Germans in the field of rocketry – were delighted to take possession of von Braun, his team and their work, although they had to act fast to retrieve the data and some of the intact V-2s, because under the Yalta agreement the area was due to be handed over to the Soviets.

The original intention of the US military was merely to debrief their German scientists and send them home. However, the War Department soon decided that here was a resource that would be useful in the longer term. Cordell Hull, the US Secretary of State,

A V-2 rocket. Both the US and USSR recruited Nazi rocket scientists for their own national defence needs, conveniently ignoring their participation in any war crimes. War criminals of no use found themselves on trial at Nuremberg.

approved the transfer of von Braun's team to the USA in June 1945. His decision was endorsed by President Harry Truman in 1947 (after von Braun had been in the USA for over a year), and 126 of von Braun's team were transferred to Fort Bliss, Texas, under the so-called Operation Paperclip. The War Department was fairly open about the process and announced to the press that: "In order that this country may benefit fully from [German progress in science] a number of carefully selected scientists and technologists are being brought to the United States. These individuals have been chosen from those fields where German progress is of significant benefit to us."

The US authorities were less transparent about many of these scientists' backgrounds.

The V-2 production facility at Kaunstein in northern Thuringia. Despite the deaths of thousands of slave labourers during the building of the facility, the Americans protected the head of the project, Wernher von Braun, after the war.

Truman had expressly stated that anyone found "to have been a member of the Nazi Party and more than a nominal participant in its activities, or an active supporter of Nazism or militarism" would be excluded from the scheme. Indeed, it was against US law for Nazi officials to emigrate to the USA. There can be no doubt that von Braun and most of his team fell into Truman's prohibited category. Von Braun had been a member of the Nazi Party and the SS, an organization declared illegal by the International Military Tribunal at Nuremberg. Von Braun later claimed that he had joined the Nazi Party because he had been told to do so, and that his work at Peenemünde had "attracted attention

at higher and higher levels. Thus, my refusal to join the Party would have meant that I would have to abandon the work of my life. My membership in the Party did not include any political activity." Yet he had been involved in Nazi organizations from almost the moment they took power. He had gained his pilot's licence from the National Socialist Aviation Corps in 1933, was a member of the *Deutsche Arbeitsfront* (German Labour Front) and of

A line of German prisoners on the Eastern Front. German military resistance to Hitler was noticeably absent during the *Wehrmacht*'s victories in 1939–41; it was amazing how subsequent defeats galvanized oppsition!

course was a member of the SS (he attended SS riding school twice a week). One can contrast his behaviour with his colleague Walter Dorenberger, whose only Nazi affiliation was membership of a hunting club.

not decisive. Samuel Klaus, the State Department representative on the JIOA, claimed the entire first batch of scientists were "ardent Nazis". The JIOA was well aware of von Braun's membership of the SS, and one report even concluded that the "subject is regarded as a potential security risk". All the visa requests were denied. The head of the JIOA, Samuel Bev, was furious and he and the newly formed CIA's director Allen Dulles had the scientists' files rewritten before being investigated once again by the FBI and State Department. Von Braun's file was changed: "No derogatory information is

> ## "It is the opinion of the Military Governor that he may not constitute a security threat"

available on the subject. It is the opinion of the Military Governor that he may not constitute a security threat to the United States." Thus von Braun was cleared of any involvement in war crimes. Indeed, some 200 Nazi scientists were similarly protected from extradition orders to stand trial at Nuremberg. It is clear Truman knew nothing of this process, and he believed that he was telling the truth when he told the Soviets at Potsdam that Nazi scientists were not working in the United States. The Soviets knew otherwise, of course, and had plenty of their "own" ex-Nazis working in the USSR on similar projects.

What is clear, however, is the massive contribution von Braun and his team made to the US rocket and space programme. Initially they trained military and academic personnel in the intricacies of rocket and missile technology, and managed to

True to Truman's intentions, the War Department's Joint Intelligence Objectives Agency (JIOA) and the FBI investigated the scientists' backgrounds. The conclusions reached by these agencies were nothing if

refurbish and launch a number of V-2s shipped from Germany, signalling the start of the US space programme. For 15 years they worked on rockets for the US Army, and after to moving to the Redstone Arsenal near Huntsville, Alabama, in 1950 they produced the Jupiter ballistic missile. In a modified form this rocket put the satellite Explorer 1 into space in 1958. In 1960 von Braun's rocket development centre was transferred from the army to the newly formed National Aeronautics and Space Administration (NASA) to work on the giant Saturn rockets. Von Braun became director of NASA's Marshall Space Flight Center and in that role was chief architect behind the Saturn V launch vehicle, the super-booster that put American astronauts on the moon. In 1970 he became a deputy to

> ## *It seemed expedient to overlook these matters in the light of the Cold War*

Auf einem Gefechtsstand in Afrika, Frühjahr 1943 (links Freiherr v. Broich)

Tafel 7

the director of NASA and head of strategic planning. He retired two years later and died in 1977, an American citizen since 1955, a man who had been absolutely central to the US space programme and undeniably an American hero.

It is clear that elements of the US War Department and CIA conspired to hide the Nazi backgrounds of scientists such as Wernher von Braun from the US president, immigration officials and the whole War Crimes' apparatus at Nuremberg. These men had often committed terrible crimes – von Braun is at the very least guilty of furthering the Nazi prosecution of the war and displaying a staggering indifference to the

One German officer whose courage, both moral and physical, was of a high calibre: Graf Claus Schenk von Stauffenberg (right), who took a leading role in the July 1944 Bomb Plot and, like many others, paid with his life.

workers at the *Mittelbrau-Dora* complex – yet such was their ability or usefulness it seemed expedient to overlook these matters in the light of the rapidly developing Cold War. In return the United States received the talents and loyalty – as von Braun said on changing his nationality in 1955: "My country has lost two world wars. Next time I would like to be on the winning side" – of some of the most talented scientists and engineers of the twentieth century, who made an immeasurable contribution to US military and technological progress. The moral ambiguities involved are perhaps best summed up by the probably apocryphal story about von Braun proudly guiding John F. Kennedy around Cape Canaveral. One aide commented in the president's ear: "Dear old Wernher, he hasn't had so much fun since he showed Hitler around Peenemünde."

The above example represents a conspiracy on the part of the Allies to protect what were essentially Nazi war criminals from justice. This not only made somewhat of a mockery of the War Crimes Tribunal at Nuremberg, it was also a slur on the memory of those individuals who had resisted the Nazi regime before and during World War II.

Another conspiracy was that undertaken by Vatican and Swiss financial institutions, which acted as conduits for SS funds to support Nazi war criminals in their flight from justice after 1945. Though such claims may be difficult to substantiate, senior Nazis did disappear after May 1945, and their whereabouts have never been identified. Such was the case with Martin Bormann, head of Hitler's secretariat, and Joseph Mengele, the Auschwitz doctor in charge of racial experiments.

GERMAN OPPOSITION

As we have seen, German opposition to Hitler was not animated by clear-cut motives or integrated by common activities. Acts of opposition ranged widely, from distributing leaflets, to conducting sermons critical of the regime to an attempted *coup d'état*. Those who participated were few in number but, interestingly, they were heterogeneous. They included aristocrats and workers, disenchanted youths and outraged bishops, civil servants and generals. The motives for resisting Hitler varied from the political and economic to the fundamentally ethical. In all

probability, the dominant motivation was ethical. Resistance within the churches sprang from a variety of motives ranging from Hitler's anti-Christian sentiments, his aggressive militarism to his killing of the

General Ludwig Beck, another German officer who was a consistent opponent to Hitler, who forced him to resign in 1938. His failing health precluded him from taking an active role in the Bomb Plot, but he was still killed for his beliefs.

hereditarily sick. The social democrats opposed him because the one-party dictatorship was the antithesis of humanitarianism and political progress. Similarly, the communists viewed fascism as an inalienable, ideological enemy.

German youth opposed National Socialism for the authoritarian rigidity that was introduced into everyday life. Many conservatives and soldiers viewed Hitler as a vulgar parvenu who didn't belong in "polite" society. Many were ultimately sickened by his treatment of Jews and other groups, both in Germany and in the occupied territories after war broke out in 1939. There was not an overarching resistance that could claim common roots and antecedents. Ultimately, in a police state built on coercion and fear, this was one of its major weaknesses.

> ### *Resistance entails the decision to step out of existing communities*

Despite Germany's extensive left-wing organizations, strong Christian heritage and aristocratic traditions, a coherent, massed and sustained opposition never emerged that looked likely to challenge seriously the Nazi regime. In part this was due to the terroristic and quasi-militaristic police system dominated by the Gestapo and SS. However, there was also widespread conformity and a base of support from all sections of society. In a memorandum written as late as 1944, Adam von Trott indicated widespread passivity among workers and little expectation of mass backing for a Putsch against Hitler. In contrast to the resistance movements in occupied territories, conspira-

torial leadership in Germany worked from the premise that large sections of the population continued to support Hitler. Not surprisingly, this uncertainty undermined German thinking and planning. To overstate the importance of resistance runs the risk of obscuring the uncomfortable reality of National Socialism's popular appeal. German resistance to Hitler was a tragic failure; it cannot be argued that the realization of the Nazis' fundamental ideological objectives were any way blunted by resistance activity. This book started from that axiomatic position.

THE JULY BOMB PLOT

Nevertheless, recent research has revealed the increasingly ambiguous reality of resistance in which affirmation and resistance become interwoven, and sharply defined differences between resisters and Nazis become blurred. The image of resistance was replaced by a more refined methodological model that sought to explore a multi-faceted response to Nazism – from cooperation, affirmation, self-defence, dissent and outright resistance. As a result, historians began to look more critically at the role of institutional actors such as "the church", "the military", "the bourgeoisie", "the working class" and so on. Resistance entails the deliberate decision to step out of existing communities in order to challenge the regime. The decision to do this – to resist – is not necessarily spontaneous, but can take place over a period of time and in response to a series of events. The individual may also undergo different forms of non-conformist behaviour that leads ultimately to resistance. What then is the difference between resistance and discontent? It is often suggested that what distinguishes the two is the conscious intention to overthrow the regime. Others would define it more precisely as the opposition against the violence of the regime wherever and whenever

it occurred. To refuse to become involved in the violence of the Nazi state, to oppose those who tolerated it and to work towards destroying it – this is resistance.

Ten years after Stauffenberg's unsuccessful assassination attempt and Hitler's settling of account with the resistance movement, Theodor Heuss, the President of the Federal Republic of Germany, made the following statement: "The 20th of July stands in a different context in that it involves the fate of other victims, the many thousands whose rejection of Hitlerism resulted in brutal physical assaults in the concentration camps, in death … the moral

A fiasco the Nazis later turned into a myth: the November 1923 Munich Beer Hall Putsch. Given a lenient sentence by a right-wing judge and treated like a celebrity in Landsberg prison, Hitler became a national political figure.

element in the group associated with the 20th of July was its basic cohesive force, in some cases more and in others less religious in nature. But the emotional element was integrated in their rational considerations. One could also choose the political and psychological aspect: groups that had previously been separated by social origin or ideology came

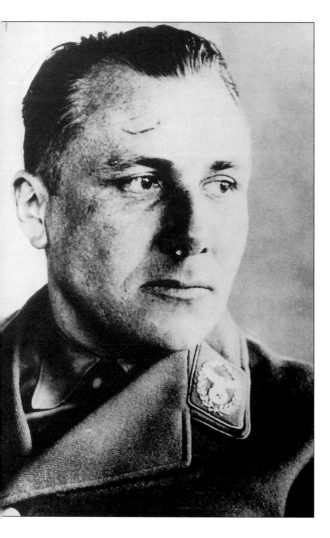

Martin Bormann, one of the senior Nazis who disappeared at the end of the war and was never seen alive again. Were Swiss and Vatican financial institutions involved in aiding the escape of Nazis from justice?

together in a bond of human trust ... The shame which Hitler imposed on us as Germans was washed away from the sullied German name by their blood. This legacy is still effective, the obligation has not yet been removed."

For many Germans in the post-war reconstruction period, the story of "resistance"

proved a powerful antidote to the horrors revealed in the name of Nazism and accusations of collective guilt for its misdeeds. Considerable discussion has taken place since the end of the war as to whether the aims put forward by the various resistance groups should be viewed as progressive or reactionary.

FORMS OF RESISTANCE

In 1946, Winston Churchill referred to the resistance movement in Germany as one of the noblest in the political history of mankind, and went on to say that their deeds and sacrifices underpinned the foundation for rebuilding the German nation. In reality, German resistance to National Socialism had little influence on the shape of the post-1945 Germanies. While the resistance may have demonstrated to the world the existence of "another Germany", the victorious Allies looked upon it with suspicion. One of the reasons for fighting the war to the finish and accepting only "unconditional surrender" was the Allied desire to shape the future of Germany and not to repeat the mistakes made after World War I. For the most part, those Germans who were entrusted with implementing key decision-making were not active in the resistance – although some had been in captivity or exile. While the resistance movement was largely unsuccessful and uncoordinated, it has become visible in terms of its dead. Those men and women have, in turn, become a memorial, a kind of national "roll-of-honour" for humanitarian values that refused to be dimmed or crushed by the brutal barbarism of Hitler and National Socialism.

In the final analysis, the fact that there was a resistance to Hitler and National Socialism – and that it was made up of different groups with different motives – has contributed to the process of coming to terms with the German past.

BIBLIOGRAPHY

Balfour, M. *Withstanding Hitler in Germany 1933–45* (London, 1988)

Balfour, M. and Frisby, J. *Helmuth Von Moltke* (London, 1972)

Conway, J.S. *The Nazi Persecution of the Churches 1933–45* (London, 1968)

Fest, J. *Hitler* (London, 1974)

Gellately, R. *The Gestapo and German Society* (Oxford, 1991)

Geyer, M. and Boyer, J.W. (eds.) *Resistance Against the Third Reich, 1933–1990* (Chicago, 1992)

Hassell, Ulrich von *The Von Hassell Diaries 1938–1944* (London, 1948)

Hoffmann, P. *The History of the German Resistance 1933–45* (London, 1977)

Hoffmann, P. *Hitler's Personal Security* (London, 1979)

Hoffmann, P. *Stauffenberg: A Family History , 1905–1944* (Cambridge, 1996)

Hohne, H. *The Order of the Death's Head. The story of Hitler's SS* (London, 1981)

Jacobsen, H.A. (ed.) *Germans Against Hitler. July 20, 1944* (Wiesbaden, 1969)

Kershaw, I. *Popular Opinion and Political Dissent in the Third Reich: Bavaria 1933–45* (Oxford, 1983)

Kershaw, I. *Hitler: volume 1, Hubris, 1889–1937* (London, 1998)

Kershaw, I. *Hitler: volume 2, Nemesis, 1938–45* (London, 2000)

Large, D.C. (ed.) *Contending with Hitler. Varieties of Resistance in the Third Reich* (New York, 1991)

Nicosia, F.R. and Stokes, L.D. (eds.) *Germans against Nazism. Non–Conformity, Opposition and Resistance in the Third Reich* (Oxford, 1990)

Kramarz, J. *Stauffenberg: The life and death of an Officer* (London, 1967)

Merkl, P. *Political Violence Under the Swastika* (Princeton, 1975)

Merson, A. *Communist Resistance in Nazi Germany* (London, 1985)

Peukert, D. *Inside Nazi Germany. Conformity, Opposition and Racism in Everyday Life* (London, 1993)

Prittie, T. *Germans Against Hitler* (London, 1964)

Reynolds, N. *Treason was no Crime. Ludwig Beck, Chief of the German General Staff* (London, 1976)

Ritter, G. *The German Resistance. Carl Goerdeler's Struggle Against Tyranny* (London, 1958)

Robertson, E.H. *Christians Against Hitler* (London, 1962)

Roon, G. van *German Resistance to Hitler. Count Moltke and the Kreisau Circle* (London, 1971)

Rothfels, H. *The German Opposition to Hitler. An Appraisal* (Chicago, 1962)

Schlabrendorff, F. von *The Secret War Against Hitler* (Boulder, 1994)

Scholl, I. *The White Rose. Munich 1942–43* (Middleton, 1983)

Schulte, T. *The German Army and Nazi Policies in Occupied Russia* (Oxford, 1989)

Steffahn, H. *Stauffenberg* (Hamburg, 1994)

Steinberg, L. *Not as a Lamb: The Jews against Hitler* (Farnborough, 1970)

Welch, D. *The Third Reich. Politics and Propaganda* (London, 1993)

Welch, D. *Hitler. Portrait of a Dictator* (London, 2000)

Whalen, R.W. *Assassinating Hitler. Ethics and Resistance in Nazi Germany* (London, 1993)

Wheeler–Bennett, J.W. *The Nemesis of Power. The German Army In Politics 1918–45* (London, 1964)

Yad Vashem, *Jewish Resistance During the Holocaust* (Jerusalem, 1971)

Zahn, G.C. *German Catholics and Hitler's War. A Study of Social Control* (London, 1963)

INDEX